SLAVERY AND THE LITERARY IMAGINATION

Slavery and the Literary Imagination

Edited by Deborah E. McDowell and Arnold Rampersad

THE JOHNS HOPKINS UNIVERSITY PRESS
BALTIMORE AND LONDON

© 1989 The Johns Hopkins University Press
All rights reserved
Printed in the United States of America

The Johns Hopkins University Press, 701 West 40th Street,
Baltimore, Maryland 21211
The Johns Hopkins Press Ltd., London

Originally published in 1989 as Selected Papers from
the English Institute, 1987, New Series, No. 13
Johns Hopkins Paperbacks edition, 1989

Contents

Introduction

The session on "Slavery and the Literary Imagination" at the 1987 English Institute emerged from an original desire on our part to have the community of scholars pay closer attention to the body of writing known as the slave narratives. At the same time, we recognized that the importance of slavery to American literature goes far beyond those narratives. The lively response to our search for speakers helped to redefine our subject for us. Not only the slave narratives but the topic of slavery itself in its profound impact on the national literature became the true center of the enterprise. Accordingly, this volume attempts to recognize something of the breadth and depth of that impact by its analysis of the work of several writers, both white and black, including former slaves, who span more than a hundred years of American literature down to our own time.

Slavery has been a grand inspiration to many of our popular writers and many of our more complex literary figures. It can hardly be a coincidence that perhaps the most influential of all American novels, *Adventures of Huckleberry Finn,* as well as what is arguably the finest American novel of the twentieth century, *Absalom, Absalom!,* are in significant ways meditations by their authors on the meaning of this institution to American life. If the latter is not a popular book, there is abundant evidence elsewhere of the hold of slavery on the national imagination. Some years ago, the historian Willie Lee Rose remarked on the intriguing fact that perhaps the three most spectacularly successful publishing events in American history—the appearances of *Uncle Tom's Cabin, Gone with the Wind,* and *Roots,* in a span of over a hundred years—were all concerned with the depiction of slavery.

For many readers, slavery undoubtedly is for the most part romance, complete with stereotypical characters and distinctive costumes. For the more sensitive, it is the American heart of darkness, the historic national sin that no holy water will ever wash away, the stony fact that denies many claims about the purpose and the nature of the historic American experiment. Less colorfully, slavery is perhaps the central intellectual challenge, other than the Constitution itself, to those who would understand the meaning of America. Slaves were not mentioned in the Declaration of Independence or the Constitution as laid out by the "Founding Fathers," but—the power of other factors notwithstanding—it was surely the bitter debate about the place of slavery in America that finally split the Republic in the middle of the nineteenth century, brought carnage and death during the Civil War on a scale unprecedented in our history, and almost destroyed the nation.

Central to the literature of slavery, we believe, must be the stories of the slaves themselves. More than one hundred slave narratives were published before the end of the Civil War, under varying and sometimes controversial circumstances. From the start, the field was mired in arguments about the authenticity of these books and their depiction of bondage, about whether they were actually written by slaves and ex-slaves or were mainly pernicious frauds by the enemies of an institution indispensable to Southern culture. Few people, however, questioned the power of these books, for they were effective weapons in the struggle against slaveholders. After the war, the production of slave narratives did not cease (although, as William L. Andrews points out in this volume, their basic vision and strategies changed). Marion Wilson Starling has estimated that just over six thousand former slaves left behind their stories of bondage and freedom, some published as late as the 1940s. Some ex-slaves granted interviews, others collaborated on, or wrote, books and essays about their experience.

Perhaps because the narratives were firmly tied in the antebellum years to the abolitionist movement, the most enthusiastic claims for their quality came from abolitionists. In 1849, the Unitarian minister Ephraim Peabody of Boston, writing with a mixture of nationalist pride and sorrow, hailed the arrival of a "new department" in world literature in the form of the slave narrative. That these narratives were superior to the general fiction of the day accounted, in Peabody's analysis, for their soaring popularity. But he also saw the "new department" as having all the essential ingredients for great literature: "We know not where one who wishes to write a modern Odyssey could find a better subject than in the adventures of a fugitive slave." To his fellow clergyman the transcendentalist Theodore Parker, the slave narratives were vastly superior to "the white man's novel" in terms of their originality and their ability to capture "all the original romance" of the American people.

American literary critics in succeeding decades did not rush to endorse Parker's judgment. For most of their existence the slave narratives have enjoyed only the most negligible status as pieces of literature, even as fiction about slavery—written mainly by whites—remained respected and admired, and in certain cases even revered. In addition, the critical reputation of these narratives was hardly stronger among blacks than among whites. However, beginning in a sense with Charles H. Nichols's landmark study *Many Thousand Gone: The Ex-Slaves' Account of Their Bondage and Freedom*—published in 1963 in Europe—the current of opinion slowly but steadily shifted, so that our understanding of the slave narrative has now reached a commendable level of sophistication. The most far-reaching claim for them has come from certain contemporary Afro-American theorists, such as Henry Louis Gates, Jr., who have argued that these narratives provided the basic paradigm for virtually all later fiction and autobiography by black Americans.

The story of the acceptance of the slave narrative as a subject worthy of critical discourse is a kindergarten melodrama compared to the story of the various interpretations of slavery offered by contending camps of historians. This historiographical Babel has been reflected in the contrasting and conflicting visions of slavery offered by our creative writers, from the romanticizing vision of the nineteenth-century white artist John Pendleton Kennedy in his *Swallow Barn* (1832) to the severe assessment by the contemporary black poet and novelist Sherley Anne Williams in her *Dessa Rose* (1986). Frank apologists for slavery, such as Thomas Nelson Page, have had their say, as have rigid opponents among poets and writers of fiction, from Harriet Beecher Stowe to George Washington Cable in the nineteenth century and Arna Bontemps in the twentieth.

Between the extremes, it seems safe to say, have fallen the majority of white writers, including Faulkner and William Styron—and not a few blacks. Many of the latter accepted the notion of slavery as a kind of fortunate fall, by which ignorant and heathenish Africans were introduced to Christ and civilization. After the Civil War, many striving blacks elected to join the forces of political conciliation between North and South and deliberately downplayed the hellish picture of slavery common in abolitionist rhetoric before the war. Others conspired, for one reason or another, with nostalgic treatments of slavery then popular. Slavery became in general the backdrop for exercises in the false dignification of black life through broad comedy and thin pathos. The reaction to such approaches may be seen in landmark works such as W. E. B. Du Bois's *The Souls of Black Folk*, which sought passionately to restore a just understanding of slavery, and even in a novel such as *Absalom, Absalom!*, in which Faulkner's vision of slavery defies easy characterization but clearly gives little aid to those who would view slavery in a nostalgic or otherwise romantic fashion, or see it as the morally justifiable basis for a regional culture.

Without any attempt at systematic coverage, but offered in a generally chronological order according to the main texts discussed, the essays in this volume permit the reader to follow the evolution of important aspects of the interplay between slavery and the American literary imagination, from Frederick Douglass's *Narrative* to Williams's *Dessa Rose*. The emphasis is on the work of Afro-American writers, but substantial attention is also paid to novels by Harriet Beecher Stowe and Lydia Maria Child. If little space is devoted to other important American writers—such as Melville, Mark Twain, Faulkner, and Styron—it is mainly because the literature on their work is already extensive. Moreover, it is our hope that ideas and approaches generated in these essays will be applied to other texts, so that a more accurate and comprehensive sense of the subject will emerge.

In "The Founding Fathers—Frederick Douglass and Booker T. Washington," James Olney examines the relationship between perhaps the two leading figures of the Afro-American nineteenth century. A former slave, Douglass wrote three autobiographies, including the most influential of all slave tales, *Narrative of the Life of Frederick*

Douglass, an American Slave, Written by Himself (1845). Booker T. Washington, born a slave but emancipated while still a boy, succeeded Douglass in the eyes of many blacks and whites as the preeminent black spokesman on the American scene. Washington's autobiography *Up from Slavery* chronicles his rise from slavery to the position of head of Tuskegee Institute, which he founded, and describes his apparently ever-expanding influence as the friend of rich industrialists and powerful political leaders, including the president of the United States. Olney shows how Washington's drive for identity and power involved an intriguing engagement of ideas and images featured in Ben Franklin's autobiography, the acquisition after slavery of a surname (Washington) that echoed the exalted task of nation building the ex-slave had set himself, and a subtle but patricidal (or regicidal) attack on Frederick Douglass.

"Changing the Letter: The Yokes, the Jokes of Discourse, or, Mrs. Stowe, Mr. Reed" reflects Hortense Spillers's belief that, in a real sense, "'slavery' is *primarily* discursive, as we search vainly for a point of absolute and indisputable origin, for a moment of plenitude that would restore us to the real, rich 'thing' itself before discourse touched it." She approaches Harriet Beecher Stowe and the contemporary Afro-American novelist and satirist Ishmael Reed as two "impression-points in the articulation of the institution of 'slavery' with a national literary identity." Without intending a search for analogues or other correspondences between the two writers, she aligns them the better to isolate and identify the repertory of strategies which each writer brings to the meditation on slavery—Stowe in what we might call a "primary" position, Reed in a signifying challenge to her discursive acts.

For William Andrews in his essay "The Representation of Slavery and the Rise of Afro-American Literary Realism, 1865–1920," slavery and freedom were the dominant themes of nineteenth-century Afro-American literature both before and after the Civil War and emancipation. However, these themes were often treated quite differently in the two periods. Before the war, slavery was depicted as a hell on earth, a perverse, obscene, and highly destructive force that threatened to annihilate the selfhood of the slave. After the war, in contrast, slavery increasingly came to be seen as a kind of crucible in which the humanity of the black man or woman was tested and, indeed, validated. Andrews notes that most of the authors of these later books did not flee the South during slavery but remained to reach some sort of compromise with the institution. The main aim of these autobiographies is not to defend slavery but to reconstruct the image of the blacks who endured it and survived with their individual dignity intact.

In "Lydia Maria Child's *A Romance of the Republic:* An Abolitionist Vision of America's Racial Destiny," Carolyn Karcher examines Child's proposal in her 1867 novel of a vision of the racial destiny of America in the aftermath of slavery and the Civil War. This vision sprang from Child's inveterate hatred of slavery and racism and from her devotion to the cause of abolitionism. Her opposition to slavery went back more than forty years before the publication of *A Romance of the Republic,* to documents such as her 1833 *Appeal in Favor of That Class of Americans Called Africans.* Unafraid to take on the forbidden topic of miscegenation, which she had treated in her 1824 novel *Hobomok,* Child had consistently attacked laws forbidding it. Miscegenation became, as Karcher puts it, "her chief metaphor for the egalitarian partnership of America's diverse races to which she summoned her compatriots in *A Romance of the Republic."*

Arnold Rampersad examines W. E. B. Du Bois's classic work *The Souls of Black Folk* (1903) as a response to Booker T. Washington's *Up from Slavery* (1901). Du Bois's book contained a direct and sustained attack on Washington, who by that time was unquestionably the most powerful black leader in the United States. Intellectually, Washington's power derived from the gospel of accommodation and compromise he preached to blacks, who were not to insist on their civil rights—especially the right to vote—in the face of hostile white Southern opposition. Rampersad argues that Washington, shunning slavery (and history in general), deliberately downplays its reality and its effects in order to reinforce the shallow and materialistic optimism of his *Up from Slavery.* Du Bois, on the other hand, delves deeply into slavery (and into history) in order to demonstrate conclusively his sense of the complexity of the Afro-American experience and his emphasis on the worthiness of black culture because of its largely unacknowledged contributions to America of music, spirituality, and toil. The contrasting attitudes toward slavery result also in contrasting attitudes on the part of the writers, and on the part of those who thought like them, toward literary form.

Hazel Carby's "Ideologies of Black Folk: The Historical Novel of Slavery" begins with her statement of a paradox: while slavery seems to be central to the imagination of the black writer, there are relatively few novels of slavery in Afro-American literature. She sees three possibilities in explanation: first, the determining influence of slave narratives on all subsequent black fictional discourse; second, the persistence of social and economic conditions of neo-slavery in black American life; and, third, the development of "an ideology of the 'folk' that comes from fictional representations of sharecropping." The principal aim of her essay is to investigate the last of these three categories, keeping in mind at all times the distortions that result from a critical will to conflate slavery with sharecropping, the nineteenth century (and earlier) with the twentieth, the rural with the urban. Arna Bontemps's *Black Thunder* and Margaret Walker's *Jubilee* are the main texts examined, but significant reference is also made to the movie versions of *The Color Purple* and *Gone with the Wind.*

In "Negotiating between Tenses: Witnessing Slavery after Freedom," Deborah E. McDowell reads Sherley Anne Williams's *Dessa Rose,* one in a growing number of contemporary novels about slavery by Afro-American writers. According to McDowell, the novel "confronts the inescapably ideological contingencies of all discourse, including itself," and "dramatizes the complex and shifting network of social and historical realities that influence the who, what, when, and where" of witnessing slavery. Such might easily be said of all the essays in this volume.

DEBORAH E. MCDOWELL
University of Virginia

ARNOLD RAMPERSAD
Columbia University

SLAVERY AND THE LITERARY IMAGINATION

James Olney

The Founding Fathers—
Frederick Douglass and
Booker T. Washington

I want to begin by commenting on the title that I insisted upon for this paper, in particular the punctuation of the title, by way of approaching my contribution to this volume. The three elements of my title ("Founding Fathers," "Frederick Douglass," "Booker T. Washington") are separated by a dash, with "Fathers" on one side, "Douglass" and "Washington" together on the other side. I insisted on this exact form of the title, but the elements could be separated by different punctuation—a comma, for example, or a colon. If separated by a comma, the title would mean that I proposed to talk about the relationship of Douglass and Washington, perhaps a relationship of continuity or of contrast, with such figures as Thomas Jefferson and Benjamin Franklin and James Madison and George Washington—those men associated with the Declaration of Independence and the U.S. Constitution who are commonly referred to as the Founding Fathers of the American nation. If separated by a colon, on the other hand, Douglass and Washington would be in apposition to Founding Fathers, and the title would suggest that I intended to talk about Douglass and Washington as themselves Founding Fathers, perhaps of a literary tradition, perhaps of an Afro-American community or nation. In any case, a comma suggests a relationship that looks backward in time from Douglass and Washington; a colon, a relationship that looks forward. But a dash—or so it seems to me, and this is what I intended—serves the purposes of both comma and colon and points to a relationship backward and a relationship forward: back from Douglass and Washington, forward from Douglass *to* Washington and forward from both of them to something else.

Both Douglass and Washington produced autobiographies; indeed,

Douglass produced three autobiographies and Washington, two or three, depending on what one takes to be an autobiography. That fact is far from insignificant, and I want to focus my observations on autobiography considered as a literary, historical, and cultural production. I have argued elsewhere, and will briefly repeat the argument here, that among the many different determinants of autobiographical form and intention there is one that we might briefly describe as "national." It is interesting and altogether pertinent that critics of various nationalities claim autobiography as a form uniquely their own. Thus, French critics claim that autobiography is a peculiarly French writing practice, Germans claim that it is peculiarly German, the English say that it is English—and I trust that I need not mention the United States because we all *know* that autobiography is peculiarly and essentially a New World form, an American way of recollecting, reorganizing, and transforming experience, and that however we may choose to define the American literary tradition, autobiography lies at the very heart of it (and also, certainly, at the very heart of the Afro-American literary tradition). Each of the nations I mentioned, moreover (and others besides, I am sure), not only claims autobiography as its own special mode but each in addition puts forward a sort of archetypal figure as *le vrai, der echt,* the real, genuine, quintessential autobiographer, the one whom all other autobiographers would imitate and equal if only they could: Jean-Jacques Rousseau for the French (or, at a later date, perhaps Michel Leiris), Goethe for the Germans, Wordsworth, I should think, for the English. For the United States the national autobiographer would undoubtedly be Benjamin Franklin: in his book a literary tradition has not only its beginning but almost its fullest, most typical example as well; his is an *exemplary* text in many different senses. And one has only to think of the differences between Franklin on the one hand and Rousseau, Goethe, and Wordsworth on the other to imagine some of the literary consequences that ensue upon adopting Franklin's book as the prototypical American life-story. But there is another document—or more precisely, another document within a document, an autobiography within an autobiography—that, as James M. Cox has convincingly demonstrated, has an equal claim to be called *The Great American Autobiography*. I am referring, of course, to the original text of the Declaration of Independence—the text as he wrote it embedded in Thomas Jefferson's *Autobiography*. Here the terms of reference are somewhat expanded, for while one might say figuratively that in writing his own life-story Franklin was also writing the general and comprehensive American story—the American Myth, if you like—of the self-made man, in the case of Jefferson the expression is more literal than figurative. Jefferson includes the Declaration of Independence, the founding document and the proleptic history of the American nation, as an essential part of his life-story.

I want to leave these two founding fathers for a moment and move across the dash of my title to the first of my founders of a different tradition—a tradition that both is and is not alien to the tradition of Franklin and Jefferson. If Benjamin Franklin is par excellence the autobiographer of the American nation, then Frederick Douglass represents the same for the Afro-American nation. In his 1845 *Narrative*, which I take to be the greatest of the slave narratives and the most completely representative, embodying virtually every convention by which we can define and recognize the slave narrative, Douglass produced a document no less astonishing than the documents of Jefferson and Franklin and bearing claims as a founding document equal to the claims of those two earlier national autobiographies. Douglass's book fits both comfortably and uncomfortably within that general American autobiographical tradition begun by Franklin—the story of the self-made man who, in telling that story, produces a kind of how-to book—and one reason that it is not altogether at ease in the Franklinesque tradition is, paradoxically, that it is also allied to the Jeffersonian tradition of autobiography. Moreover, while Douglass's *Narrative* is both within and against the Franklinesque tradition, it similarly begins another, alternative, tradition as it sets and points the course for black American writers from Booker T. Washington and W. E. B. Du Bois and James Weldon Johnson down to Richard Wright and Malcom X and Ralph Ellison and beyond. The *Narrative* is thus formally determined by being in a reasonably well established line of American autobiographies, but it is more specifically determined because it is in a line of *black* American autobiographies and, I would say, non-autobiographies as well.

The comfort/discomfort with which Douglass's book fits in the Franklinesque tradition is evident even in its title: *Narrative of the Life of Frederick Douglass* . . . [here I permit myself an ellipsis that will be filled in later] *Written by Himself.* The original title of what we know as Franklin's *Autobiography* was *Mémoires de la vie privée de Benjamin Franklin, écrits par lui-même* (1791). Later the book appeared as *The Private Life of the Late Benjamin Franklin . . . Originally Written by Himself, and Now Translated from the French* (1793), and, in the same year, as *Works of the Late Doctor Benjamin Franklin: Consisting of His Life Written by Himself, Together with Essays, Humorous, Moral, and Literary, Chiefly in the Manner of the Spectator.* Observe that the recurrent tag—"écrits par lui-même," or "Written by Himself"—is also a part, and an essential part, of Douglass's title (and it is also a part of the titles of slave narratives by Olaudah Equiano, William Grimes, Solomon Bayley, Jarena Lee, William Hayden, Leonard Black, William Wells Brown, Henry Bibb, Henry "Box" Brown [in one version], Nancy Prince, William Green, William J. Anderson, John Thompson, Noah Davis, Reverend G. W. Offley, and Harriet Jacobs). But that simple tag and apparently bland assertion, "written by himself," carries infinitely greater meaning when made an integral part of the title by Douglass or Bibb or W. W. Brown or Harriet Jacobs than when it is tacked on to Franklin's text by an editor or publisher after the author's death. The world was well aware that Franklin was capable of producing a written account of his life if he chose to do so; after all, he was a signatory of the document that declared freedom and independence for an emergent nation and one of the authors and a signatory of the Constitution of that nation. But it was never intended that Douglass or Bibb or Brown or Jacobs should be able to read and write and thus have the capacity to produce and publish the narratives of their lives and, in an act analogous to the writing of the Declaration of Independence, declare freedom and independence for themselves. And it is, of course, altogether significant that on the occasion of his first abortive attempt at escape, Douglass wrote passes for himself and his fellow slaves—passes to freedom, as it was intended, "written by himself." In the hand of Frederick Douglass, "written by himself" is not an incidental and insignificant addition to the title but is an immensely proud claim, the claim of someone who is as much a self-made man as Benjamin Franklin—someone, indeed, vastly more self-made than Franklin. Douglass's *Narrative* is structured as a chiasmus and at the very center of the text, where the arms of the "chi" cross, we find this chiastic sentence, introducing the self-creative and self-liberating fight with Edward Covey: "You have seen how a man was made a slave; you shall see how a slave was made a man." Through the power of his narrative, as through his resistance to Covey's "nigger-breaking" tactics, Douglass calls himself from nonexistence into existence, the "onlie begetter" of his own manhood. What had Franklin to show that would compare with this?

But "written by himself" is even more than a proud claim. It is an act of linguistic assertion and aggression, in the language and the literary mode of the oppressor, and it is doubly so: it is explicitly an act of assertion and aggression against the slaveholders who tried to prevent the slave's ever learning to read and write; and it is implicitly an act of assertion and aggression against abolitionists who were too often inclined to confuse sponsorship with authorship and to take possession of "their" ex-slaves in a manner not altogether unlike the original possession by slaveholders. At least, I think this is the effect of "Written by Himself" in Douglass's case, and I believe that it was his insistence that he was and would continue to be the author of the narrative of his life that caused Douglass's quarrel and ultimate break with William Lloyd Garrison and the Garrisonians. Whether he foresaw this or not (and it is questionable whether either Franklin or Jefferson could have foreseen the same in their cases), Douglass established a tradition of *writing* with his *Narrative* as well as giving an account of upholding a tradition of resistance to oppression. "Written by Himself" certifies that Douglass has authored his own existence in much the same way that naming his own postslavery name as the last words of the text certifies his identity against any and all who might threaten it. "I subscribe myself, Frederick Douglass" are the final words of the text, and thus he surrounds the story of his life with "himself" and "myself"–"written by Himself" and "I subscribe myself"–with Frederick Douglass and Frederick Douglass, a completed circle enclosing and securing the narrative chiasmus of his life.

I promised earlier to fill in the ellipsis that I permitted myself in the title of Douglass's *Narrative*. The full title of his book reads *Narrative of the Life of Frederick Douglass, an American Slave, Written by Himself.* The restored phrase "an American slave" stands in dramatic counterpoint to "Written by Himself"; a slave is a chattel, after all, not a human being, and a chattel is incapable of a narrative "Written by Himself." Moreover, within the phrase itself–"an American Slave"–the key words "American" and "Slave" are, as it were, yoked by violence together, and they present the most radical, the most aggressive, the most thoroughgoing challenge imaginable to the very idea of the American nation and to the Declaration of Independence that proclaimed and summoned into existence the "United States of America."

I noted earlier that one reason (not the only one, however) that Douglass's book is not entirely in the mold of Franklin's book is that it has ties to a Jeffersonian tradition as well. What I meant was that the *Narrative,* while it is the account of a self-made man, is also, and in the highest degree, a revolutionary document, for the man who here makes himself begins not just in a lowly social position but in a condition of bondage, of oppression, of chattel slavery, and becoming free requires the breaking of bonds, the overthrow of the oppressor and enslaver. To put it briefly, Douglass's *Narrative* is a declaration of independence, with echoes of the earlier national document, and while Franklin signed that earlier document, it was Jefferson alone who wrote it ("written by himself," as it were) and included it in his *Autobiography.* "We hold these Truths to be self-evident, that all Men are created equal, that they are endowed by their Creator with certain unalienable Rights, that among these are Life, Liberty, and the Pursuit of Happiness. . . . But when a long Train of Abuses and Usurpations, pursuing invariably the same Object, evinces a Design to reduce them under absolute Despotism, it is their Right, it is their Duty, to throw off such Government, and to provide new Guards for their future Security." What else but this are all the slave narratives about, and Douglass's supremely so? At issue was whether the violent paradox of Douglass's title—"an American Slave"—should continue to be a part of the life of the nation or whether, even before it was issued, the Emancipation Proclamation should be effectively subjoined to the Declaration of Independence.

Surely Douglass knew exactly what he was doing when he iron-ically, but in dead seriousness, echoed the final phrases and rhythms of the Declaration in the concluding sentence of his own declaration. Here is the conclusion to the national Declaration: "We, therefore, the Representatives of the United States of America, in General Congress, Assembled, appealing to the Supreme Judge of the World for the Rectitude of our Intentions, do, in the Name, and by Authority of the good People of these Colonies, solemnly Publish and Declare That these United Colonies are, and of Right ought to be, Free and In-dependent States. . . . And for the support of this Declaration, with a firm Reliance on the Protection of divine Providence we mutually pledge to each other our Lives, our Fortunes, and our sacred Honor." And here is the conclusion to the specific declaration of independence and freedom for the community of American slaves: "Sincerely and earnestly hoping that this little book may do something toward throw-ing light on the American slave system, and hastening the glad day of deliverance to the millions of my brethren in bonds—faithfully rely-ing upon the power of truth, love, and justice, for success in my hum-ble efforts—and solemnly pledging myself anew to the sacred cause,—I subscribe myself, FREDERICK DOUGLASS."[1] Concluding the narrative account of his progress from slavery to freedom, which is strikingly like the Declaration's account of the abuses and the oppressions of the king of England and the necessity therefore to break free and become an independent nation, Douglass pledges, subscribes, and signs himself as Franklin, Jefferson, and other signatories of that earlier, parallel but alien document had pledged, subscribed, and signed themselves. What had been written into the founding document of the nation but then renounced and denied as soon as written in—"that all Men are created equal," with an unalienable right to "Life, Liberty, and the Pursuit of Happiness"—had to be rewritten and reasserted by Frederick Douglass as the founding father of the Afro-American nation. In his reassertion of the idea of the nation, both American and Afro-American, Douglass produced a kind of Ur-text of slavery and freedom that, whether individual writers were conscious of imitating Douglass or not, would inform the Afro-American literary tradition from his time to the present.

One person who *was* conscious of Douglass, of what he had done and of what he represented as a founding father, was Booker T. Washington, and precisely because he was conscious of Douglass as well as supremely aware of who he was himself, where he was, and where he wanted to be in the shifting black and white worlds of his time, Washington had to develop a highly complex set of strategies that would serve to relate him both to the founding fathers of the American nation and, at the same time but in rather a different way, to Frederick Douglass himself—whom Washington seemed often to want to claim as his own father (for Washington's father was unknown to him) but perhaps only so that he could use or misuse him as sons are sometimes said to do with their fathers. And to complicate matters for Washington, there was another man around, younger than Washington himself (which, for Washington, only made the situation more hazardous) and altogether willing to displace Washington as the true son and heir of Douglass: I mean, of course, W. E. B. Du Bois. But before I look at the tangle of Washington, Du Bois, and Douglass I would like to consider Washington's relationship to, or his appropriation of, the more distant founding fathers of the American nation.

Critics have occasionally noted Benjamin Franklin's presence in Washington's *Up from Slavery*, and it is scarcely surprising that a book bearing that title should resemble in local passages as well as overall structure the first great account of making it through one's own efforts in America. Richard B. Bernstein, in his recent and attractive book *Are We to Be a Nation? The Making of the Constitution* gives some sense of the nearly unbounded possibilities and promise available to Americans—that is, to white male Americans—in the eighteenth century: "It was possible for the tenth son of a Boston tallow

chandler, a runaway apprentice, to come to Philadelphia virtually penniless and eventually become wealthy, respected, and powerful—this
was the achievement of the great Dr. Franklin, who became a symbol
of the possibilities of America to his admiring compatriots."[2] Building on this most American of myths and starting out in even more des-
perate circumstances than Franklin, Washington naturally produced a
text that at many points echoed Franklin's originary version of the
American success story. The passage in *Up from Slavery* most frequently cited for comparison with Franklin's *Autobiography* is the account of Washington's arrival in Richmond on his way to the
Hampton Institute, an account that runs parallel precisely to the following description of Franklin's arrival in Philadelphia:

> I have been the more particular in this Description of my Journey, and
> shall be so of my first Entry into that City, that you may in your Mind
> compare such unlikely Beginnings with the Figure I have since made
> there. I was in my Working Dress, my best Cloaths being to come round
> by Sea. I was dirty from my Journey; my Pockets were stuff'd out with
> Shirts and Stockings; I knew no Soul, nor where to look for Lodging. I
> was fatigu'd with Travelling, Rowing and Want of Rest. I was very hungry,
> and my whole Stock of Cash consisted of a Dutch Dollar and about a Shil-
> ling in Copper. . . .
>
> Thus I went up Market Street as far as fourth Street, passing by the
> Door of Mr. Read, my future Wife's Father, when she standing at the
> Door saw me, and thought I made as I certainly did a most awkward ri-
> diculous Appearance. Then I turn'd and went down Chestnut Street and
> part of Walnut Street. . . . I walk'd again up the Street, which by this time
> had many clean dress'd People in it who were all walking the same Way; I
> join'd them, and thereby was led into the great Meeting House of the Quak-
> ers near the Market. I sat down among them, and after looking round a
> while and hearing nothing said, being very drowzy thro' Labour and want
> of Rest the preceding Night, I fell fast asleep, and continu'd so till the Meet-
> ing broke up, when one was kind enough to rouse me. This was therefore
> the first House I was in or slept in, in Philadelphia.[3]

Washington's arrival in Richmond, according to his own account,
was, if anything, even less propitious than Franklin's in Philadelphia,

but then his ascent, starting from so far down, could also be the greater:

> By walking, begging rides both in wagons and in the cars, in some way, after a number of days, I reached the city of Richmond, Virginia, about eighty-two miles from Hampton. When I reached there, tired, hungry, and dirty, it was late in the night. I had never been in a large city, and this rather added to my misery. When I reached Richmond, I was completely out of money. I had not a single acquaintance in the place, and, being unused to city ways, I did not know where to go. . . .
>
> I must have walked the streets till after midnight. At last I became so exhausted that I could walk no longer. I was tired, I was hungry, I was everything but discouraged. Just about the time when I reached extreme physical exhaustion, I came upon a portion of a street where the board sidewalk was considerably elevated. I waited for a few minutes, till I was sure that no passersby could see me, and then crept under the sidewalk and lay for the night upon the ground, with my satchel of clothing for a pillow. . . .
>
> In order to economize in every way possible, so as to be sure to reach Hampton in a reasonable time, I continued to sleep under the same sidewalk that gave me shelter the first night I was in Richmond. Many years after that the coloured citizens of Richmond very kindly tendered me a reception at which there must have been two thousand people present. This reception was held not far from the spot where I slept the first night I spent in that city, and I must confess that my mind was more upon the sidewalk that first gave me shelter than upon the reception, agreeable and cordial as it was.[4]

But this is not the end of Washington's bemused contemplation of how far—and only in America—he has risen; that Franklin could (in Bernstein's words) "come to Philadelphia virtually penniless and eventually become wealthy, respected, and powerful" is nothing to the story of Washington, but a few years removed from slavery, coming to Richmond and then coming *back* to Richmond years later "respected and powerful" indeed.

> As I write the closing words of this autobiography I find myself—not by design—in the city of Richmond, Virginia: the city which only a few

decades ago was the capital of the Southern Confederacy, and where, about twenty-five years ago, because of my poverty I slept night after night under a sidewalk.

This time I am in Richmond as the guest of the coloured people of the city; and came at their request to deliver an address last night to both races in the Academy of Music, the largest and finest audience room in the city. This was the first time that the coloured people had ever been permitted to use this hall. The day before I came, the City Council passed a vote to attend the meeting in a body to hear me speak. The state Legislature, including the House of Delegates and the Senate, also passed a unanimous vote to attend in a body. In the presence of hundreds of coloured people, many distinguished white citizens, the City Council, the state Legislature, and state officials, I delivered my message, which was one of hope and cheer; and from the bottom of my heart I thanked both races for this welcome back to the state that gave me birth. (P. 385)

It was probably not lost on Washington that three of the most important of the Founding Fathers—George Washington, Thomas Jefferson, and James Madison—were Virginians; it was certainly not lost on him that Richmond was the capital of an illegitimate nation, founded precisely to undo the work of union accomplished by those true Founding Fathers.

Other Franklinesque touches are to be found throughout *Up from Slavery*, from the discourse on the civilizing properties of the toothbrush and a daily bath to homilies on the means to self-improvement and the schedule that Washington himself followed to that end. But one of the most interesting instances of Franklin's presence in Washington's text is not this sense of one exemplary, exhortatory document following upon another but rather the appearance of Franklin's name in the altogether classic first sentence of Washington's autobiography: "I was born a slave on a plantation in Franklin County, Virginia." Washington did not choose the county of his birth any more than he chose the condition of slavery for that event, but he did choose to put both of those items in the first sentence of an autobiography that would call to the minds of many readers the autobiography of the famous Dr. Franklin of Philadelphia. That he was born in Franklin County, Virginia, is for Washington like an *objet trouvé* for artists of a certain persuasion: it was a found felicity that Washington would make yield whatever it possessed of value for his story. On the other hand, when it comes to choosing a postslavery name, it is not a question of an *objet trouvé*, to make of what one can, but rather of an *objet cherché et choisi—bien cherché, soigneusement choisi*. Before coming to a description of his choice of a name for himself, Washington tells of the general way in which freed slaves chose names at the time of emancipation:

> In some way a feeling got among the coloured people that it was far from proper for them to bear the surname of their former owners, and a great many of them took other surnames. This was one of the first signs of freedom. When they were slaves, a coloured person was simply called "John" or "Susan." There was seldom occasion for more than the use of one name. If "John" or "Susan" belonged to a white man by the name of "Hatcher," sometimes he was called "John Hatcher," or as often "Hatcher's John." But there was a feeling that "John Hatcher" or "Hatcher's John" was not the proper title by which to denote a freeman; and so in many cases "John Hatcher" was changed to "John S. Lincoln" or "John S. Sherman," the initial "S" standing for no name, it being simply a part of what the coloured man proudly called his "entitles." (P. 226)

"This was one of the first signs of freedom," Washington says, and surely few moments, few choices, could be as crucial as this one. John Adams, at another highly significant moment of freedom, wrote in his 1776 essay *Thoughts on Government*, "You and I, my dear Friend, have been sent into life, at a time when the greatest law-givers of antiquity would have wished to have lived. How few of the human race have ever enjoyed an opportunity of making an election of government more than of air, soil, or climate, for themselves or their children." How few also, as Booker Washington himself observed, have had the opportunity of naming themselves, and not with just any old name, not even with the name of just any one of the Founding Fathers, but with the name of the one who would be called the Father of his Country. "My second difficulty," Washington says of his starting to school, was with regard to my name, or rather *a* name. From the time when I could remember anything, I had been called simply "Booker." Before going to school it had never occurred to me that it was needful or appropriate to have an additional name. When I heard the school-roll called, I noticed that all of the children had at least two names, and some of them indulged in what seemed to me the extravagance of having three. I was in deep perplexity, because I knew that the teacher would demand of me at least two names, and I had only one. By the time the occasion came for the enrolling of my name, an idea occurred to me which I thought would make me equal to the situation; and so, when the teacher asked me what my full name was, I calmly told him "Booker Washington," as if I had been called by that name all my life; and by that name I have since been known. . . . I think there are not many men in our country who have had the privilege of naming themselves in the way that I have. (Pp. 231–32)

"An idea occurred to me which I thought would make me equal to the situation"—it is really quite a wonderful moment and an equally wonderful account. Washington had no reason subsequently to regret his choice of name—on the contrary. When he says, "I calmly told him 'Booker Washington,' as if I had been called by that name all my life; and by that name I have since been known," there is a clear sense of pride and satisfaction about the name he has chosen. But had he been faced with this opportunity and necessity to choose a name at certain later moments in his life, I think Washington would have had a more difficult time deciding on one from among at least three different names: "Washington" would certainly have remained attractive, but at a later date "Franklin" might have seemed equally attractive and so also, at other times and for quite other reasons, "Douglass" might have presented itself as a possibility. "Booker T. Franklin" or "Booker T. Douglass"—well, it was not to be, but the mere suggestion tells us something of the greater complexity of Washington's relationship to founding predecessors.

While I think that Washington would not in fact have adopted Douglass's name for his own and would hardly have thought of it except perhaps for a brief time in his youth, it did become extremely important to Washington to establish himself as Douglass's heir and legitimate successor as *the* leader in the Afro-American community, not indeed as a Founding Father of freedom, for the time of that founding was past, but as an inheritor of the mantle—and one who would be more than capable of filling out the heroic proportions of that garment. If, as I have implied, Douglass's 1845 *Narrative* can be seen to correspond in American/Afro-American history to the Declaration of Independence, then I think one might say that *Up from Slavery*, as a founding document, corresponds in many ways to the U.S. Constitution. The *Narrative* and the Declaration are revolutionary documents in a way that *Up from Slavery* and the Constitution are not (and I should say that Douglass yielded nothing of his revolutionary determination in *My Bondage and My Freedom* [1855]; consider, for example, the fierce appendix to that book called "What to the Slave is the Fourth of July?"). Yet the framers of the Constitution were seeking to build a government based on the principles of the Declaration, just as Washington knew that in order to be successful as the founder of the Tuskegee Institute and the Tuskegee Machine he had to claim, or to seize, the authority of his great founding predecessor. And it was vastly important for Washington, as it was not for Douglass or the framers of the Declaration, that his succession to power be—or at least seem to be—legitimate. Slaveholders' claims have no legitimacy in Douglass's *Narrative*, just as the English king's claims have no legitimacy in the Declaration; but Washington clearly could not proceed in this revolutionary mode in his time and his place and given his temperament and intentions. Douglass, like the framers of the Declaration, could be wholeheartedly and uncompromisingly revolutionary; Washington, like the framers of the Constitution, had no option but conciliation if he was to unite the disparate groups to which he appealed. Douglass was the Great Revolutionary, Washington the Great Compromiser, and as Justice Thurgood Marshall has reminded us, if we need reminding, the Constitution of the United States came into being only as a result of what has been termed the Great Compromise—that compromise that accepted slavery and the three-fifths-of-a-human-being status of slaves without once mentioning slaves or naming slavery anywhere in the document.

If Washington was to found an educational institution and a base of power in Alabama, he had to placate the white South and establish a state of compromise with white Southerners; at the same time, if he was to draw the black community together behind him, he had to appropriate Douglass to his purposes rather than reject or behead him. At least, I believe that he felt it was necessary to do this at first, for there seem to be two distinct phases to Washington's treatment of Douglass, the first in *Up from Slavery* (1901) and in Washington's biography of Douglass (1907), the second in *My Larger Education*, published in 1911 when Douglass had been safely dead for sixteen years. Indeed, in this later book, Washington comes perilously close to rejecting and beheading the Founding Father when, describing his own great success in the speech he delivered at the Atlanta Exposition—a speech that is included official and entire in *Up from Slavery* and that caused observers and correspondents to hail Washington as the Douglass of his day and the Moses of his people—Washington lays side by side these two terse and factual, but at the same time highly interpretative and intimately related, sentences: "Frederick Douglass died in February, 1895. In September of the same year I delivered an address in Atlanta at the Cotton States Exposition" (p. 424). This is close to open patricide, or, perhaps, regicide, although it is not customarily the regicide himself who proclaims, "Le roi est mort; vive le roi!" The more common technique with Washington, however, especially early on, is to identify himself with Douglass but to do so very carefully and only with a Douglass who has been interpreted in such a way that he appears from the beginning to be little different from Washington himself.

Henry Adams, in sending a copy of the privately published edition of *The Education of Henry Adams* to his old friend Henry James, described his autobiography thus: "The volume is a mere shield of protection in the grave. I advise you to take your own life in the same way, in order to prevent biographers from taking it in theirs."[5] Biography is thus homicide, and autobiography is suicide. I do not want to claim that Washington thought or acted according to the radically and intensely ironic mode of Henry Adams, but I do think that from

Adams's formulation we can understand something of the strategic uses to which Washington put both biography and autobiography. Adams might think that writing an autobiography would provide a "shield of protection in the grave," but Washington was not to be swayed from his determination to take Douglass's life in his way by the mere fact that Douglass had taken his own life, and presumably in *his* way, not just once but three times. Washington, biographer and autobiographer, proceeded to take Douglass's life anyhow and very much according to his own desires and needs.

When appropriating Douglass in a relatively benign way, Washington at times does so, interestingly enough, by coupling him with his own namesake, George Washington, thus merging patronymics, lineal descent, and legitimate inheritance very effectively. In a circular, "Appeal in Behalf of the Frederick Douglass Home," sent out from Tuskegee Institute in January 1909, Washington asks that "Negro fraternal organizations, churches and Sunday schools throughout the country" set aside February 14 to celebrate Douglass's birthday and "that systematic collections be taken to the end that we may wipe out this indebtedness of $4,800 and make Cedar Hill a Mecca for our people as Mount Vernon is to the white people of the country." Again, in *Up from Slavery* Washington tells two anecdotes to illustrate his point about the proper conduct of race relations when, as he puts it, one race is "less fortunate" than the other. "This reminds me," Washington writes,

> of a conversation which I once had with the Hon. Frederick Douglass. At one time, Mr. Douglass was travelling in the state of Pennsylvania, and was forced, on account of his colour, to ride in the baggage-car, in spite of the fact that he had paid the same price for his passage that the other passengers had paid. When some of the white passengers went into the baggage-car to console Mr. Douglass, and one of them said to him: "I am sorry, Mr. Douglass, that you have been degraded in this manner," Mr. Douglass straightened himself up on the box upon which he was sitting, and replied: "They cannot degrade Frederick Douglass. The soul that is within me no man can degrade. I am not the one that is being degraded on account of this treatment, but those who are inflicting it upon me." (P. 267)

On the same question, Washington continues,

> My experience has been that the time to test a true gentleman is to observe him when he is in contact with individuals of a race that is less fortunate than his own. This is illustrated in no better way than by observing the conduct of the old-school type of Southern gentleman when he is in contact with his former slaves or their descendants.
>
> An example of what I mean is shown in a story told of George Washington, who, meeting a coloured man in the road once, who politely lifted his hat, lifted his own in return. Some of his white friends who saw the incident criticised Washington for his action. In reply to their criticism George Washington said: "Do you suppose that I am going to permit a poor, ignorant, coloured man to be more polite than I am?" (Pp. 267–68)

One might remark that the Douglass anecdote, according to Washington's account, was transmitted viva voce, thus implying a certain closeness between the two men as well as a confirmation from the older man of Booker T. Washington's attitudes toward race relations. Beyond that, it is a compelling strategy on Washington's part to bring together the man from whom he would assume leadership and the man from whom he assumed a name.

Following Henry Adams's dictum about biography and autobiography, Washington often adopts the strategy of appropriating Douglass's life to his own and of incorporating and revising Douglass's text in the text of his—Washington's—life. Thus when, in *Up from Slavery*, Washington comes to describe his first trip to Europe, the alert reader will naturally be reminded of Douglass's account of a similar crossing from America to Europe some fifty-four years earlier. Lest the reader miss the connection, Washington tells how, on the return voyage, he one day found himself in the ship's "fine library," and what book should fall into his hands but—*mirabile dictu*—"a life of Frederick Douglass, which," Washington continues,

> I began reading. I became especially interested in Mr. Douglass's description of the way he was treated on shipboard during his first or second visit to England. In this description, he told how he was not permitted to enter the cabin, but had to confine himself to the deck of the ship. A few min-

utes after I had finished reading this description I was waited on by a committee of ladies and gentlemen with the request that I deliver an address at a concert which was to be given the following evening. And yet there are people who are bold enough to say that race feeling in America is not growing less intense! At this concert the Hon. Benjamin B. Odell, Jr., the present governor of New York, presided. I was never given a more cordial hearing anywhere. A large proportion of the passengers were Southern people. After the concert some of the passengers proposed that a subscription be raised to help the work at Tuskegee, and the money to support several scholarships was the result. (P. 368)

Not only have times changed, one seems to hear Washington saying, but a man of the hour, who knows that to prosper you must "cast down your bucket where you are," is founding a great work in Tuskegee that goes altogether beyond the vision of Frederick Douglass.

The exceedingly bland biography of Douglass that Washington published in 1907 is interesting not so much for its inherent quality as a biography—we would not today go to it for Douglass's biography—as for the circumstances of its authorship and what its production tells us about Washington himself. The book was one in a series called "American Crisis Biographies" and at one point (in November 1903) had been assigned to W. E. B. Du Bois to write. *The Souls of Black Folk* had been published earlier in the same year (in April), the quarrel between Du Bois and Washington was just coming to a head, and Washington, who apparently had something like a first right of refusal to write the biography, declined to let this prize fall to his chief rival as heir apparent to Frederick Douglass. Having offered the assignment to Du Bois, the editor of the series of biographies (Ellis Oberholtzer) had to write Du Bois that Washington insisted on the assignment for himself, "and it was in vain that I endeavored to have him take an assignment to some character illustrating a later period in the negro's development, some freedman, a period he knows very well, and one that calls for less historical learning."[6] We will never know what Du Bois might have done with the biography of Douglass, but we know what Washington did, which was precious little. He sat on the biography and kept it for himself—or, more precisely, kept it away from

Du Bois—but coming away from Washington's biography of Douglass one has a very different sense of the subject than one has coming away from, say, Douglass's own 1845 *Narrative* "Written by Himself." Washington concludes his account of the crucial fight with Covey, for example, by remarking that "it speaks well for the natural dignity and good sense of young Douglass that he neither boasted of his triumph, nor did anything rash as a consequence of it, as might have been expected from a boy of his age and spirit."[7] The Douglass of Washington's biography is not exactly given to compromise, but he is no revolutionary either.

It is very clear to a reader familiar with Douglass's three autobiographies that Washington wrote his biography entirely out of the latter two and, it appears to me, more out of the final version, *Life and Times of Frederick Douglass,* than out of the middle one, *My Bondage and My Freedom.* In *My Larger Education* Washington writes, "I heard so much about Douglass when I was a boy that one of the reasons why I wanted to go to school and learn to read was that I might read for myself what he had written and said. In fact, one of the first books that I remember reading was his own story of his life, which Mr. Douglass published under the title of 'My Life and Times.' This book made a deep impression upon me, and I read it many times" (pp. 422–23). Presumably Washington, with his reference to "My Life and Times," has in mind the *Life and Times of Frederick Douglass,* but that book was first published in 1881—the same year that Tuskegee Institute was founded by the twenty-five-year-old Booker T. Washington—and thus could not have been "one of the first books" read by the boy. It was a slip of the pen, no doubt, where *My Bondage and My Freedom* (1855) or, less likely, *Narrative of the Life of Frederick Douglass* (1845) was intended, but a significant and revealing slip all the same, for the Douglass of the *Life and Times* is much more Washington's Douglass than the Douglass of either of the earlier volumes of autobiography. The revolutionary fervor of his first two exercises in autobiography was largely spent by the time Douglass wrote his postbellum third autobiography, and such revolutionary spirit as remains in that very long book is diffused and without much force. This is Washington's

Douglass, a man much more akin to Washington himself and much more manageable by the Tuskegean. This was the largely tamed Douglass who was induced to give a commencement address at Tuskegee in 1892 that sounds as if it might have come straight from Washington's pen, and whose journey through the South on that occasion—where he would go and when, and, even more, where he would *not* go—was stage-managed with great care by the Founder of the Tuskegee Institute Himself.

Consider the matter for a moment from Washington's point of view in, say, 1905 or 1910. Douglass had no doubt been a great man and a glorious example to those in slavery, but his day was past, and, in any case, Washington was not in slavery, or certainly did not feel himself so. As John Hope Franklin has said, "By the beginning of the new century, Washington was one of the most powerful men in the United States."[8] For such a man, in such a position, what was Douglass's legacy? In itself it was nothing; its value lay altogether in what Washington could make of it. If he could establish his claim as Douglass's legitimate successor and inheritor, he would have the allegiance of a great many blacks otherwise suspicious of him and his intentions. But put the question another way, still, however, from Washington's point of view: If Douglass was a Founding Father, what had he ever founded of any lasting significance? He had founded his own freedom and, perhaps, by his example the freedom of a few others. But this obviously would not be a satisfactory answer or a sufficient ambition for Washington. I imagine that Washington would be happy that Founder's Day is still celebrated every year at Tuskegee, more than one hundred years after his founding of the institute.

I have been looking backward and laterally rather than forward in the matter of "The Founding Fathers—Frederick Douglass and Booker T. Washington," but perhaps it will suffice to say that a number of critics of Afro-American literature—Houston A. Baker, Jr., Henry Louis Gates, Jr., and Robert B. Stepto, to name only three—have demonstrated brilliantly that it is precisely this revisionary playing-off against, or signifying on, previous texts that constitutes literary history and, specifically, the Afro-American literary tradition.

There is a continual playing-off against, or signifying on, the texts of the Founding Fathers of the American nation, particularly on the subjects of slavery and freedom, in writers from Frederick Douglass to Richard Wright and Ralph Ellison and beyond (and of course the same thing in many white American writers as well); and there is also the continual playing-off against, or signifying on, previous texts within the Afro-American tradition. It seems to me that with the fine work already done and still being done, I do not need to elaborate on this aspect of my subject, so I will simply return to my beginning and say that my title looks in two directions and that Douglass and Washington are at that point where the two directions meet, cross, and recross.

CODA

I am acutely aware that the tradition of writing and the tradition of reference, appropriation, and influence that I have been tracing is exclusively male. It might be pointed out that neither the Declaration of Independence nor the Constitution of the United States bears the signature of a woman; indeed, women are treated in those two documents in ways not dissimilar to the treatment of slaves—that is to say, as if they did not exist except for purposes of taxation and calculating proportionate representation. Moreover, until very recently, writings by black women have suffered the same fate as the writings of black men, but even more drastically and entirely: disregard, neglect, rejection, denial. It is only in the past few years, for example, that Harriet Jacobs's *Incidents in the Life of a Slave Girl* has been shown to be an authentic slave narrative and a genuine autobiographical text rather than the work of the white abolitionist Lydia Maria Child.

Putting aside the male exclusivity in the founding of the American nation and in the shaping of an Afro-American literary tradition (this latter taking the form in my essay of a line from Frederick Douglass, Booker T. Washington, W. E. B. Du Bois, and James Weldon Johnson down to Richard Wright, Malcolm X, Ralph Ellison, and beyond), it is interesting and timely to speculate on another line in Afro-American writing, composed of black women writers, a line that runs parallel to the Douglass-Washington–Wright-Ellison line but that also signifies on and revises that exclusively male tradition. Just as one might claim that Douglass is a kind of Founding Father of an Afro-American literary tradition, so one could say that Harriet Jacobs and Elizabeth Keckley, among others, are Founding Mothers of another Afro-American literary tradition that includes among its major figures Zora Neale Hurston, Alice Walker, Toni Morrison, and Gloria Naylor. In interesting ways, the autobiographies and novels of Jacobs, Keckley, Hurston, Walker, Morrison, and Naylor share similarities with one another that they do not share with the autobiographies and novels of Douglass, Washington, Du Bois, Johnson, Wright, Malcolm X, and Ellison. On the other hand, just as the line established by Douglass and Washington is not unrelated to the founding documents of the American nation, so the Jacobs-Keckley line is not unrelated to the Douglass-Washington tradition. On the contrary, it bears to that sometimes parallel, sometimes merging and crossing, line the most intimate sort of relationship by way of questioning, commentary, critique, revision, supplementation, reorientation, and reimagination.

The way in which writing by black women both complements and criticizes writing by black men might be pointed up by mention of one clear difference in typical themes in the two lines: autobiographies and novels in the Douglass-Wright tradition are almost entirely concerned with the encounter between the races and with the efforts of black males to realize themselves or to make something significant of their lives in a world where whites rule and oppress blacks. Autobiographies and novels in the Jacobs-Hurston tradition, on the other hand, while they situate themselves in that same world where whites rule, are much less concerned with racial encounters than with sexual encounters, much more trained on the relationships of men and women, whether black or white, than on the relationships of the races, black and white. As emblematic of this complementarity in dissimilarity, one might mention Hurston's *Their Eyes Were Watching God* on the one hand and Wright's *Black Boy* on the other. Hurston's novel was published some eight years before Wright's book and so cannot properly be said to contain a critique of Wright's vision; nevertheless, the social, cultural, and linguistic richness that informs Hurston's book can be seen as the expression of a vision and tradition contrary to and critical of the vision and tradition of bleakness and barrenness, hostility and utter hopelessness, that *Black Boy* conveys. And it is altogether pertinent to remark that while there is never anything positive about sexuality in *Black Boy* (Bess, the girl in Memphis, for example, represents for the protagonist nothing more positive than another of the traps laid by the South to hold him in its toils), *Their Eyes Were Watching God* holds out sexual promise and sexual fulfillment as emblems and proof of the greatest possible good in a universe where human beings, should they miss out on that sexual promise and fulfillment, are condemned to a life of Job-like suffering.

The present remarks are intended only as a note, not a new essay, but they point to a subject that is complex, rich, and deep and one that is well worth pursuing at length.

NOTES

1. *Narrative of the Life of Frederick Douglass, an American Slave, Written by Himself,* edited and with an introduction by Houston A. Baker, Jr. (New York: Viking Penguin, 1982), 159.

2. Richard B. Bernstein, *Are We to Be a Nation? The Making of the Constitution* (Cambridge: Harvard University Press), 3–4.

3. *The Autobiography of Benjamin Franklin,* ed. Leonard W. Labaree, Ralph L. Ketcham, Helen C. Boatfield, and Helene H. Fineman (New Haven: Yale University Press, 1964), 75–76.

4. *The Autobiographical Writings,* vol. 1 of *The Booker T. Washington Papers,* ed. Louis R. Harlan and John W. Blassingame (Urbana: University of Illinois Press, 1972), 239–40. Hereafter, quotations from *The Autobiographical Writings* are cited parenthetically in the text.

5. *Letters of Henry Adams, 1858–1918,* 2 vols. ed. Worthington C. Ford (Boston: Houghton Mifflin, 1930–38), 2:495.

6. *The Correspondence of W. E. B. Du Bois,* 3 vols., ed. Herbert Aptheker (Amherst: University of Massachusetts Press, 1973), 1:63.

7. Booker T. Washington, *Frederick Douglass* (Philadelphia: George W. Jacobs, 1907), 41.

8. John Hope Franklin, Introduction to *Three Negro Classics* (New York: Avon Books, 1965), p. xi.

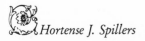 *Hortense J. Spillers*

Changing the Letter

THE YOKES, THE JOKES OF DISCOURSE,
OR, MRS. STOWE, MR. REED

The nineteenth-century phrase "peculiar institution" is richly suggestive in more than one way. If we think of "institution" as a specific sum of practices that so configure our sense of "public" and "private" that the rift between them is not as substantial as we might flatter ourselves to think, then antebellum slavery in the United States offers a preeminent paradigm of conflated motives. Its practices, upheld by an elaborate system of codes, subject to conditions of market, sanctioned by the church (in the American plurality), and generating the nation's first community of fugitives, actually sustained no private realm, even though such practices were central to the "home," to the very stuff of domesticity as planter-aristocrats envisioned it. There is no more ironic, pathetic, or is it cynical, juxtaposition of gazes that capture the attention than this scene from *Uncle Tom's Cabin*: Tom and the Master, Inc., including Augustine St. Clare, Vermont cousin Ophelia, and Evangeline St. Clare, have all just arrived at New Orleans after a trek down the Mississippi on the *Belle Rivière*. The carriage in which the party has been delivered to the "many mansions" of St. Clare, so to speak, stops in front of an ancient house,

> built in the odd mixture of Spanish and French style of which there are specimens in some parts of New Orleans. It was built in the Moorish fashion,—a square building inclosing a courtyard, into which the carriage drove through an arched gateway. The court, in the inside, had evidently been arranged to gratify a picturesque and voluptuous ideality. Wide galleries ran all around the four sides, whose Moorish arches, slender pillars, and arabesque ornaments carried the mind back, as in a dream, to the reign of oriental romance in Spain. In the middle of the court, a fountain threw high its silvery water, falling in a never-ceasing spray into a marble basin, fringed with a deep border of fragrant violets. The water in the fountain,

pellucid as crystal, was alive with myriads of gold and silver fishes, twink-ling and darting through it like so many living jewels. Around the foun-tain ran a walk, paved with a mosaic of pebbles, laid in various fanciful patterns; and this again, was surrounded by turf, smooth as green velvet, while a carriage-drive inclosed the whole. Two large orange-trees, now fra-grant with blossoms, threw a delicious shade; and, ranged in a circle round upon the turf, were marble vases of arabesque sculpture, containing the choicest flowering plants of the tropics. Huge pomegranate trees, with their glossy leaves and flame-colored flowers, dark-leaved Arabian jessa-mines, with their silvery stars, geraniums, luxuriant roses bending beneath their heavy abundance of flowers, golden jessamines, lemon-scented ver-benas, all united their bloom and fragrance, while here and there a mystic old aloe, with its strange, massive leaves, sat looking like some hoary old enchanter, sitting in weird grandeur among the more perishable bloom and fragrance around it.[1]

In puritan terms, we might imagine, the landscape of this scene is "heathen" in its excess, openly engaging the senses, and, in case we miss the point the first time, the narrator reinforces a semantics of "oriental romance" and splendor in the "dark-leaved *Arabian* jessa-mines" (emphasis mine). As though Tom "grows" out of the fictive landscape, deeply akin "by nature" to its specular vitality, we are told that he gets down from the carriage and looks around him with an "air of calm, still enjoyment." Tom is the scene's Negro, and the Negro in his fully imagined Africanity: "The Negro, it must be re-membered, is an exotic of the most gorgeous and superb countries of the world, and he has, deep in his heart, a passion for all that is splen-did, rich, and fanciful; a passion which, rudely indulged by an un-trained taste, draws on them the ridicule of the colder and more correct white race" (p. 180).

In explaining the central nervous system of the African in her *Key to Uncle Tom's Cabin*, Stowe expatiates on those symptoms of living being which are proximate to and expressive of this seductive nature; of peculiar susceptibility, the African personality's

> sensations and impressions are very vivid, and their fancy and imagination lively. In this respect, the race has an oriental character, and betrays its

tropical origin. Like the Hebrews of old and the Oriental nations of the present, they give vent to their emotions with the utmost vivacity of expression, and their whole bodily system sympathizes with the movement of their minds. . . . Like Oriental nations, they incline much to outward expression, violent gesticulations, and agitating movements of the body. . . . They will laugh, weep, and embrace each other convulsively, and sometimes become entirely paralyzed and cataleptic.[2]

Exactly *what* the "orient" is has no precision, of course, in Stowe's account, lacking specificity as a potential repertoire of geopolitical arrangements that flow together toward a cultural synthesis. It is simply *there*, in an unimpeachable unity of essential impression and in fatal binarity with the other great mythical valence of Stowe's discourse—the "Anglo-Saxon race—cool, logical, and practical."[3] The members of Tom's "African race," of "oriental character," are "in their own climate . . . believers in spells, in 'fetish and obi,' in the 'evil eye,' and other singular influences, for which probably there is an origin in this peculiarity of constitution."[4] We are called upon to imagine that competence and success of magical skill may be "accounted for by supposing peculiarities of nervous constitution quite different from those of the whites."[5]

Even though Augustine St. Clare is, as far as his status goes, a "white" man—and we are also explicitly told this by the narrator—the descriptive apparatus that surrounds him in the New Orleans scene is loaded with hints of "gorgeousness." St. Clare is, after all, "in his heart a poetical voluptuary" (p. 180). The narrative energies of this scene, in its intense physicality, are decidedly marked for the realm of the natural—forces whose symbolic resonance is "deeply connected with fertility, sexuality, and reproduction,"[6] or what Kenneth Burke identifies as the "realm of ubertas": "the realm of the appetites generally."[7] If the markings of landscape all signify the "exotic," the strange, the foreign, then what better gaze to preside over it than Tom's?—that of the gagged, bewildered, "unreading," but "read," object who representatively and representationally embodies, historically, North America's most *coveted* body, that is, the *captivated* man/woman-child who fulfills a variety of functions at the master's behest?

The horror of slavery was its absolute domesticity that configured the "peculiar institution" into the architectonics of the southern household. So complete was its articulation with the domestic economy that from one angle it loses visibility and becomes as "natural" to the dynamics of culture as "luxurious" roses "bending beneath their heavy abundance of flowers" (p. 179). Gillian Brown expresses that "peculiar" relationship in this way: "Slavery disregards [the] opposition between the family at home and the exterior workplace. The distinction between work and family is eradicated in the slave, for whom there is no separation between economic and private status. When people themselves are 'articles' subject to 'mercantile dealings,' when 'the souls and bodies of men' are 'equivalent to money,' women can no longer keep houses that provide refuge from marketplace activities."[8] Deeply embedded, then, in the heart of American social arrangements, the "peculiar institution" elaborated "home" and "marketplace" as a useless distinction, since, at any given moment, and certainly by 1850 — the year of the Fugitive — the slave was as much the "property" of the collusive state as he or she was the personal property of the slaveholder. We could say that slavery was, at once, the most public private institution *and* the ground of the institution's most terrifying intimacies, because fathers *could* and *did* sell their sons and daughters, under the allowance of *law* and the flag of a new nation, "conceived in liberty," and all the rest of it.

It seems to me that every generation of systematic readers is compelled not only to reinvent "slavery" in its elaborate and peculiar institutional ways and means but also, in such play of replication, its prominent discursive features as "a group of objects that can be talked about (or what is forbidden to talk about), a field of possible enunciations (whether in lyrical or legal language), a group of concepts (which can no doubt be presented in the elementary form of notions and themes), a set of choices (which may appear in the coherence of behavior or in systems of prescription)."[9] This field of enunciative possibilities — its horizon, its limits, its enabling postulates, and its placement in perspective with other fields of signification — constitutes the discourse of slavery, and, as concretely material as the "institution" was, as a natural historical sequence and as a scene of pulverization and murder, "slavery," for all that, remains one of the most textualized and discursive fields of practice that we could posit as a structure for attention. In a very real sense, a full century or so "after the fact," "slavery" is *primarily* discursive, as we search vainly for a point of absolute and indisputable origin, for a moment of plenitude that would restore us to the real, rich "thing" itself before discourse touched it. In that regard, "slavery" becomes the great "test case" around which, for its Afro-American readers, the circle of mystery is recircumscribed time and again. This realization is stunning: as many times as we reopen slavery's closure, we are hurtled rapidly forward into the dizzying motions of a symbolic enterprise, and it becomes increasingly clear that the cultural synthesis we call "slavery" was never homogeneous in its practices and conception, nor unitary in the faces it has yielded. But to behave as if it were so matches precisely the telos of African persons in the United States—as Tom becomes in Stowe's text *the negro*—this existence of a him/her in a subject-position that unfolds according to a transparent, self-evidentiary motif. In other words, to rob the subject of its dynamic character, to captivate it in a fictionalized scheme whose outcome is already inscribed by a higher, different, *other*, power, freezes it in the ahistorical.

The collective and individual reinvention of the discourse of "slavery" is, therefore, nothing other than an attempt to restore to a spatiotemporal object its eminent historicity, to evoke *person/persona* in the place of a "shady" ideal.

My notion of Harriet Beecher Stowe and Ishmael Reed as two impression-points in the articulation of the institution of "slavery" with a national literary identity has several parts to it: First, I intend no precise analogy on an intertextual juncture by juxtaposing these radically disparate figures of practice. In other words, I am not suggesting any explicit relationship of priority and indebtedness between textual performances in a selected spatiotemporal sequence by invoking these disjunctive literary instances. By bringing them into a posture of alignment, however, I do wish to concede textuality itself as a self-conscious systematicity that never closes, or that distributes itself in a more or less concentrated "mask of repetition." Reed is not so much "rewriting" Stowe as he is intimating a repertory of strategies that denote, that circumlocute, a particular cluster of discursive acts. In Reed's system, Stowe generates, in that regard, one set of traffic signals, we might say. Further, we are pursuing as systematically as we can what the blurbs for and the critics of *Flight to Canada* have already told us: Afro-American writers, in Richard Yarborough's words, are still striving to "distance themselves from all that *Uncle Tom's Cabin* represents."[10]

In that sense, Stowe, the writer, casts a long shadow, becomes an implacable act of precursor poetics that the latter-day black writer would both outdistance *and* "forget." The 1852 work, in its startling history of publication and, in the view of George Eliot, its "founding" of the "Negro Novel,"[11] apparently has no national precedent in its endless powers of proliferation: If we could recuperate the material and symbolic wealth that has accrued to the gross national product and somebodies' "stash" from the purported repetitions of this work's narrative and iconic treasures, we would have considerable wealth ourselves and, with it, a fairly precise analogy to the *exchange* and *use* value of the *captured* African body. Yarborough observes that "Stowe's best-seller inspired a veritable flood of Uncle Tom poems, songs, dioramas, plates, busts, embossed spoons, painted scarves, engravings, and other miscellaneous memorabilia, leading one wry commentator to observe, '[Uncle Tom] became, in his various forms, the most frequently sold slave in American history.'"[12] And in 1853, a children's version of the novel was offered under the title of *A Peep into Uncle Tom's Cabin*. The prurient, voyeuristic suggestion of "peep" is quite appropriate to a national mentality that wants to "steal" a *look* at the genitals in vague consciousness that they are covered by an interdiction.

For all its undeniable, even seductive, narrative powers, *Uncle Tom's Cabin*—both in itself and in the "fallout" it induced—might be regarded as a lethal weapon, or *because* of such powers, and for at least once in the history of literary production, we can say that we have found in this work a "poem" that *can* "kill."

Second, then, we regard *Flight to Canada*—in its absurdist, dystopian, mocking impulse—as a revisionary, corrective move that wants to speak both *for itself* and *against* something else; it seems to me that we have hold here of *forms of coexistence* in a potential configuration of slavery's discursive field: "statements [for Reed] that are no longer accepted or discussed, and which consequently no longer define either a body of truth or a domain of validity, but in relation to which relations of filiation, genesis, transformation, continuity, and historical discontinuity can be established."[13] Foucault calls this instance of *form of coexistence* a "field of memory" that might obtain between texts and their propositions. When, for instance, Reed's invention of "Mammy Barracuda" is said to have worn a "diamond crucifix on her bosom," so heavy that it forced her to stoop, and that, further, when she went into the fields once "and the sun reflected on her cross so, two slaves were blinded,"[14] we think instantly and all at once in a sort of static of "confused" imagery. At once, the dazzling cross mocks its founding icon-text in specious display and plays to a notion of *specie* translated into an equivalent materiality. "Mammy Barracuda," in her brilliant captivity, embodies an entirely oxymoronic motion—at the crossroads of wealth and exchange, she is a major player, though not a beneficiary. Wearing wealth's symptoms on her magnanimous bosom and around her neck, she is made to throw a reflection that *shatters* the sight, instead of *healing* it. This Christian "practice," in its complicated maneuvers of displacement, is refracted back on Stowe's Tom, who, according to the way the reader remembers the scene, dies in a gesture of crucifixion in the midst of "two slaves'"—Sambo and Quimbo's—act of repentance (p. 441). Although Tom's eyes are closed in the death scene by young George Shelby, a few pages after the flogging scene, we realize essentially that Tom has been murdered by hanging, which thematic recurs with the regularity of clockwork in the annals and narratives of North American enslavement. Stowe's subsequent narrative on prior texts of Scripture and the historical is absorbed and displaced in Reed's contemporary structure through his translation of syntactic elements into an iconic sign, whose "verbal equivalent . . . is not a word but a phrase or indeed a whole story."[15]

Third, if these textualities in a "field of memory" demonstrate historical and literary repetition as the radical disjuncture between "history" on the one hand and "farce" on the other, then we can say that "slavery" as a potential topic of enunciative and discursive practices, is, first and foremost, textual, or eminently constituted *in discourse*, since not only are its objects of selectability neutral, so to speak, or subject to refashioning, but the same terms can entertain different relationships provided they are inserted into different cultural axes.[16] We observe, then, certain structural homologies, or dis-homologies, that adhere between *Flight to Canada* and *Uncle Tom's Cabin*, or, more precisely, structural dis-homologies that are revealed *only* in the former instance of Reed as dissimilarity of *structure*, and not transparent prophetic utterances.

In other words, with *Flight to Canada*, we are aware that "slavery," in at least one of its dimensions, is claimed by the "lumberhouse" of "literature" and that just as Reed invades Stowe's invasion of those symptoms and appurtenances of Gothic convention, which, in Stowe, become the mythical landscape of a principle of inversion ("Simon Legree" is "really" "Augustine St. Clare" with his drawers down), "slavery" inscribes a repertoire of relationships of texts and among texts that are purely open to modes of improvisation and rearrangement.[17] These precisely segmented portions of cultural content might be defined as "cultural units," or clusters and systems of interconnected cultural units, in a system of positions and oppositions.[18]

It will be clear, then, that in reading Reed against and with Stowe, I am suggesting *Flight to Canada* as both a systematic protocol and a rereading and redoing of "slavery" and as an instance of "Quickskill," to appropriate the name of one of Reed's chief figures, which would undo the triangle of metaphysical desire[19] that has killed the "slave" in Tom endlessly. What are in Stowe the yokes and the crucifixion of discourse undergo transformation in Reed into the jokes and the liberation of discourse from systems of cultural content that, once upon a time, enslaved "9 million and more," Paule Marshall observes, in their African diaspora.

But, somehow, this is too easy; I am expected to come down on the argument in this way. I must admit that for me, an individual instance of "reader/researcher/teacher/writer," not at all entirely disparate from my identity as one of those latter-day survivors of history's nightmare, I am rather predictably selfish in my own desires—I want to eat the cake *and* have it. I *want* a *discursive* "slavery," in part, in order to "explain" what appears to be very rich and recurrent manifestations of neo-enslavement in the very symptoms of discursive production and sociopolitical arrangement that govern our current fictions in the United States. At the same time, I suspect that I occasionally resent the spread-eagle tyranny of discursivity across the terrain of what we used to call, with impunity, "experience." But I further suspect that this crucial dilemma is rather common among Afro-American scholars, who are pledged to the critical work of the *inventory* and its relationship to a community's survival. Even though we are urged to think that there is no necessary equivalence between the major prongs of the foregoing sentence, I invoke a correspondence between them inasmuch as I sense a very real and deep connection between knowledge and its maps of distribution and the economies of dominance and subordination.

In other words, I am conscious that in attempting to "read" "slavery" as it provides the thematic ground that situates these radically disparate acts, I am also critiquing my membership in at least two continuous *and* discontinuous communities of ideological interest. There is a hint of quite similar hermeneutic tensions at play in *Flight to Canada*, whose sustained chuckle over "slavery" seems to me almost always contrived and self-consciously cautious. But I am sure of one thing: Mrs. Stowe's "slavery" demarcates an inexorable grimness, which I really did not want to experience again as a reader. But I had to, while Reed's work is sufficiently interstitial that "flight to Canada," indeed, "flight," remains entirely possible. After *Uncle Tom's Cabin*, one needs a drink. Reed provides it. If these "sets of choices," translatable into the efficacies and "benign" neglects of public policy, are *virtually* a matter of words, then I see no reason *not* to choose an "out" and the best available one. In short, can Stowe be laughed to death, and is Reed the man for the job?

After contemporary feminist theory has patiently and often impressively "recovered" Harriet Beecher Stowe for a quite visible place in the canon of literary procedure we study as the "American Renaissance," the posture of the foregoing interrogation will probably strike the mind as adversarial. Even Ann Douglass's negative assessment of Stowe's work,[20] in Jane Tompkins's estimation, is significant as a countercritical move to the inherited opinions of *Uncle Tom's Cabin*, in particular. Tompkins argues in *Sensational Designs* that the effectiveness of Stowe's novel is directly measurable by its "popularity." "Written by, for, and about, women,"[21] *Uncle Tom's Cabin*, as sentimental fiction, Tompkins continues, enjoins the reader to different critical assumptions about the nature and function of literature: "In modernist thinking, literature is by definition a form of discourse that has no designs on the world. It does not attempt to change things, but merely to represent them, and it does so in a specifically literary language whose claim to value lies in its uniqueness. Consequently, works whose stated purpose is to influence the course of history, and which therefore employ a language that is not only unique but common and accessible to everyone, do not qualify as works of art."[22]

Rather, then, than aiming to dethrone Melville and Hawthorne, Tompkins would prefer to "argue that the work of the sentimental writers is complex and significant in ways *other than* those that characterize the established masterpieces."[23] The reader is asked to set aside, then, certain "familiar categories for evaluating fiction—stylistic intricacy, psychological subtlety, epistemological complexity—and to see the sentimental novel not as an artifice of eternity answerable to certain formal criteria and to certain psychological and philosophic concerns, but as a *political* enterprise, halfway between sermon and social theory, that both codifies and attempts to mold the values of its time."[24]

While I am wholly sympathetic to Tompkins's project and to that of other corrective feminist readings of *Uncle Tom's Cabin*, like Elizabeth Ammons's[25] and Gillian Brown's, I must say that in my own reading of the statements insinuated in the discourse of this novel, a feminist social paradigm is not only problematized, but made problematic in ways I had not quite expected. Because there is "noise" in the discursive field of this novel, and a path to radical social revision has not been properly cleared, though descried, the work *metaphorizes* the very dilemma of *reading* and *living* that Afro-American readers, at least—who, by the way, also come with at least *two* kinds of sexual markings, described as "female" and "male"—have palpably *felt* for over a century about *Uncle Tom's Cabin*.

One of the best readings of this novel remains, to my mind, James Baldwin's "Everybody's Protest Novel,"[26] which locates a "theological terror" at the heart of the work. It is this cultural crux that most worries my own encounter with Stowe's novel—how, for instance, a unitary reading of "slavery," "according" to the "Gospel," springs the trap of Tom's dismemberment. Even though I would falsify myself and my argument here if I did not admit right away that Baldwin's "reading woman" is, in my opinion, woefully reactionary and static, I think that he nevertheless taps a central vein of inquiry, in particular reference to black persons. I am little concerned, though, that *Uncle Tom's Cabin*, written as it was "by, for, and about women"—and that when we say as much, we do not, in our public and critical discourses, at least, *mean* to tell anything at all about the Chloes and the Topsies—represents an anti-energy for the captive woman. In the symptoms of anomie and facelessness that constitute them, these fictional cyphers are granted *no* vocality, even in this *fictive* work of woman's. Enclosed in and structured by an essential silence, Chloe and Topsy, for all their sporadic "talking," remain the carnivalesque propositions of female character who inscribe "growths" and "bumps" on the surface of Stowe's fiction. "Woman," here and elsewhere, then and now, so elides with a *revoked* adjectival marker named "white" that we barely notice. But this complex of a problematic does not concern me as much here as do the fate and career of discursive bodies, as they are buttressed "to death," as it were, by what seems to me an opportunistic deployment of the ideologies of a kerygmatic Gospel.

It is entirely possible to read the texts of a demotic (or preaching) Gospel in a subversive way, that is, in a way that does *not mandate* the sacrifice of children, or the crucifixion of black bodies, male or female. We know this, because the annals of Afro-American narratives in sermons demonstrate quite effectively, in certain notable instances,[27] how the assertions and declaratives of speech acts about words "about God"[28] conduce toward a radically different social "choreography." That Stowe "orchestrates" a thematics of sacrifice as an instance of a *posited* "necessity"; that this segment of the eschatological attaches itself to the history, or to the narratives about the history, of children and "The Negro," altogether reinforce the phallogocentric motives of slaveheld "private property" in a woman's hands, since it insists that somebody *else* pay the *price* of its own unmitigated desire. This is exactly what Reed's narrator, Quickskill, means when, outrightly assertive, he accuses the historical, here-fictionalized, Stowe of "stealing" Josiah Henson's story. Can we say that an invented "Tom," in fact, *pays* the lady's way?

Gillian Brown introduces the lexicon of "desire" to the criticism I read on *Uncle Tom's Cabin*, but Brown claims that Stowe renounces "desire" *for* and *in* woman, as episodes of the novel reflect the "imagined state of possession, that is, the condition of satiety and fulfillment, the goal of the pursuit of happiness. The nondesiring woman is therefore the embodiment of perfect ownership."[29] Inasmuch as "private property," we are told, is already compromised and sullied by the alienable, by inequality, by the violence of *retaining*, is there possibly "perfection" in it? And what is the status of this "perfection"? unless by it we mean "owning" "well" and "lots." Even Simon Legree does *that*.

This work, then, poses no pluralism of reference in its reading and interpretation of "Gospel" relating to the work's duo of major figures. If the "blueprint" for "colonizing" the "world" in the name of the "family state," under the leadership of Christian women,[30] is prefigured in this novel, then I know precisely where I belong in its domestic economies, and I want no parts of it. Stowe's view, then, is not *the* "Gospel," already an Ur-text of polyvalence, but it is just *that*, a *view*, which, in its systematic assertions—and ironically enough, this is the foundation of its powers—*rivals*, even *analogizes*, in every sense, the omnipresent and univocal narrative structures in which "slavery" continues to arise in the fiction. In short, Stowe poses a purely local and quite particularistic notion *as* the place of an imagined and fictitious "universality." But there seems deep division here, and I want to test my reading of a few of its implications. When I say "division," I mean that Stowe and some of her commentators might have been, and may be, still, satisfied that a monolithic Calvinist "god" "dictated" this work, but other readings may detect at least moments of it that reveal themselves as the slippery, unintended messengers of a different and explosive "dictation."

I want to return momentarily to the scene whose grammar I highlighted at the beginning of this essay as the ground of concatenation upon which my reading of Stowe's work might be tried. The architecture of the courtyard and the mansion of St. Clare's New Orleans estate is clearly intended as an emblematic gesture. I regard it as a central excerpt of narrative and conceptual feature that could well discover its inspiration in Catharine Beecher's *Treatise on Domestic Economy*.[31] But Stowe's sister makes it clear that as the author of the latter, she is addressing her remarks to nuclear-family heads of *moderate* means. Nonetheless, there is about this "oriental" locus of splendor and hidden cargo a didactic content that conceals a heteroclitic sexual motivation. Even if Augustine St. Clare persists in error as a disbelieving slaveholder, there is no reason why the fleshly beauties of Pontchartrain and the New Orleans place would not captivate and express the most cultivated appetitive capacities. But is its appeal to the appetite also its mischief—the mark of a decidedly prohibitive status in the system of the work?

A partial answer to this interrogation lies in the fascinating commentary on *Uncle Tom's Cabin* recently provided by Karen Halttunen, who tracks the Gothic undergirdings of Legree's Red River domain. But inasmuch as Legree and St. Clare might be accorded the same value as the twin and primary moments of the very same "domestic economy," I accede to Halttunen's apt decipherment of the close relationship between "good" and "bad" slaveholders. These figures of inversion both stand on Gothic ground, which becomes, for Ishmael Reed, late in the twentieth century, a profound metaphor of explicit sadomasochistic performance.

Halttunen shows that the appropriation of the discourse of Gothic in the hands of Harriet Beecher Stowe was preceded in the Beecher family by both her father's and brother's use of its strategies in their respective sermonic work. The Gothic literary tradition that underscored Lyman Beecher's 1825 sermon series, entitled "Six Sermons on the Nature, Occasions, Signs, Evils, and Remedy of Intemperance," goes back, Halttunen points out, fifty years to Horace Walpole's *Castle of Otronto*, among other sources. "The haunted house of the 'School of Walpole,' with its standard appointments, including heavy iron doors, trapdoors with metal rings, secret doors hidden behind tapestries, long galleries, winding staircases, underground vaults, labyrinthine passages, neighboring convents, monasteries, and charnel houses,"[32] provided similar impetus for Henry Ward Beecher's 1844 lecture series, "Lectures to Young Men, on Various Important Subjects," preached in Indianapolis. The central sermon of this series, "The Strange Woman," which offers a philippic against prostitution, comprises, in Halttunen's view, a narrative of "sexual nausea."[33] A remarkable structural similarity obtains between Stowe's paradisiacal landscape of lush gardens and her brother's sermonic narrative of the garden of seduction: "Stowe's description of St. Clare's exotic house, like her brother Henry's treatment of the Ward of Pleasure, reflected the debt of the Gothic genre to the eighteenth-century oriental tale."[34] But as the ascribed oriental sensuousness of Henry Ward Beecher's "'Ward of Pleasure' points to [*his* narrative's] Ward of Death, St. Clare's gorgeous home serves in Stowe's narrative *as a kind of way station to the ruined mansion of Simon Legree*."[35]

As though we might insinuate the sentences that attach to St. Clare's narrative into the ones that describe Legree's, we could say that St. Clare's discursive career is not finished until we gain the radical shift of geographical and ontological ground provided by the severe isolation of Legree's estate. These sentences are strangely retroversive: "What was once a smooth-shaven lawn before the house, dotted here and there with ornamental shrubs, was now covered with frowsy tangled grass, with horse-posts set up, here and there, in it, where the turf was stamped away, and the ground littered with broken pails, cobs of corn, and other slovenly remains" (p. 369). The "dark-leaved Arabian jessamines" of St. Clare's gardens reappear as Legree's ruin—as "mildewed jessamine," a "ragged-hanging honeysuckle," and "what once was a large garden . . . now all grown over with weeds . . . through which . . . some solitary exotic reared its forsaken head" (p. 369). We are teased with intimations of St. Clare, who is, indeed, "former," both as regards the *sold* mansions of New Orleans and Lake Pontchartrain and the text, with reference to so-called enlightened slaveholding: "[Legree's estate] had formerly belonged to a gentleman of opulence and taste, who had bestowed some considerable attention to the adornment of his grounds" (p. 369). It is as though we have penetrated our own dreams to their foundation in a neurotic context, wherein dream-maker and -work are engendered in the same, continuous moments of an alienated self-identity.

When Stowe places "Little Eva" and "Uncle Tom" in a new and revised "Garden of Eden," she might have aimed for a type of Eva as the mother of resurrected, reconstructed humankind, but there is nothing "pious" or "holy" about the altogether shocking outcome: The sacrificial lamb of *Uncle Tom's Cabin*—in the dual person of Eva the temptress and Tom the castrated—must be expended as *punishment* for crimes against the culture, rather than as *salvation* for the culture. Elizabeth Ammons argues that Stowe proposed "as the foundation for a new democratic era, in place of masculine authority, feminine nurture: a type of love epitomized in the Christlike girl-child, Eva, whose name calls to mind the Edenic mother of the race. Figuring as Eva's adult counterparts are several mothers and one man: sweet-tempered black Tom, meek like Christ, yet fiercely loyal to a democratic set of values. The author's obvious contradiction of gender in the Eva/Christ and Tom/heroine associations, both of which serve as savior analogues in the novel, animates her conviction, as she later stated it plainly, that 'there was in Jesus more of the pure feminine element than in any other man.'"[36]

As I see this, Stowe herself, "more manly," we might say, than "Christ-like," *did* know the *Father*, as it seems to me that the vaunted feminist gaze of this work remains deformed. I do not mean to say that "feminism," as an ideology of discourse, critique, and practice, offers a unitary response, or that it ought to, although it would be easier if there were a single and orthodox critical function that we could all appropriate as "feminism" and leave it at that. I also do not intend our current repertoire of intellectual practice and historical specificity called "feminist" to assume more import than it actually bears. In other words, Stowe's "feminism" and her critics' "feminism" need not duplicate mine in order to command their own considerable weight and time. But I am saying that the *requirements of sacrifice*, which Stowe's critics inevitably point out as death's raison d'être in the novel and which Stowe herself reinforces in the narrative's habits of pathos, seem to galvanize the murderous instincts of patriarchal, phallogocentric synthesis rather than effectively challenge them. Though much of the way one decides the issue depends on the angle from which she is seeing, I tend to agree with Eric Sundquist, who argues that Stowe "returned . . . to a paternal revolutionary tradition bound up in the wrath of God the father, to the suppressed Calvinistic vengeance of Lyman Beecher's religion to which the novel's immense moral work of mothers may finally give way."[37]

If Stowe's colonizationist vision of the millennium is embedded in a "messianic view of history," then I am not sure that the "good news" of the New Dispensation offers compatibility with an order of things "'in which all persons tend to lose their individual reality in the great cosmic drama of God's plan.'"[38] For certain, the "theological terror" of a Calvinistic, patriarchal God, the Father, the Name, the Law, is not *commensurate* with a soteriological scheme that watches the sparrow's fall and has already counted the numbers of hairs on our head. In what does this "terror" consist, this "terror" that has dictated the theft of the Negro's body, in God's name, excised his genitals in print and in fact, and hailed it under the sign of "meekness"; that abdicates from "desire" in its feminine manifestations, but recuperates it in the female child-body; and that so devalues the issue from the black female's body that we have ascribed to it *only* the potential of a wild proliferation—a "jes grew"? Who, in short, is Stowe's "Father-God," who has visited us in so much splendor of dread that even today the book generates a shudder of revulsion?

Even though we assign to the intricate involutions of St. Clare's courtyard the status of culture by virtue of a literal and exquisitely modulated "cultivation," the New Orleans scene does not escape the markings of a "nature/culture" split. "Everywhere" an invaginated surface—"a deeply fringed border of violets," for example, and enclosures that open into other recesses—threatens to overcome the planned and precise geometries of landscape gardening. The scene, loaded with suggestions of a *tamed* wildness, is repeated in reference to St. Clare's summer house on Pontchartrain:

> St. Clare's villa was an East-Indian cottage, surrounded by light verandas of bamboo-work and opening on all sides into gardens and pleasure-grounds. The common sitting room opened onto a large garden, fragrant with every picturesque plant and flower of the tropics, where winding paths ran down to the very shores of the lake, whose silvery sheet of water lay there, rising and falling in the sunbeams. (P. 281)

One of the *as if* secret places of the Lake Pontchartrain estate belongs, specifically, to Eva and Tom, "a little mossy seat, in an arbor, at the foot of the garden" (p. 281). Tompkins reads the putative visionary import of this scene as typologically paradigmatic, remarking that its "iterative nature . . . presents in miniature the structure of the whole novel."[39] This assertion is plausible, I think, but I would grant its feasibility for reasons rather to the side of Tompkins's. If, as the female of both scenes, which collide and slip into an imploded unity, Eva (alongside Tom) comes to be associated with "nature," then an explanation is not too far in the distance.

Halttunen points out that at least in the Midwest during the nineteenth century "fruits and fountains and, most significant, flowers," a euphemism for the female genitals, are situated in a grid of "enchanted objects."[40] Although Halttunen is referring here specifically to William Beckford's *Vathek* (1786) and Edgar Allan Poe's "Masque of the

Red Death" (1842), I think we can explore flowers in the Stowe landscape toward similar ends.

In fact, I would go so far as to say that Eva is fatally marked by a
lush sensuality in three distinct instances: (1) At the end of the arbor
scene, the narrator, discoursing on certain symptoms of immortality
in the spiritually precocious child, claims that the "seal of heaven" (p.
283) is upon her. This apparently unmotivated charge is here context-
ualized by Eva's intimate contact with Tom, whose "blackness" traditionally configures the site of a pollution. (2) Pages earlier, Tom, on a
typical day of St. Clare's lightly sarcastic banter-at-home, sits on "a little mossy seat in the court, every one of his button-holes stuck full of
cape jessamines, and Eva, gayly laughing, was hanging a wreath of
roses around his neck; and then she sat down on his knee, like a chip-
sparrow, still laughing" (p. 195). (3) In another scene that rehearses this
same complex of discursive and kinesic gestures, Eva has just been
told the story of Scipio by St. Clare: "A few moments, and merry
laughs were heard through the silken curtains, as Eva and St. Clare
were pelting each other with roses, and chasing each other among the
alleys of the court" (p. 255). Drawn together by certain symptoms of
domestic intimacy, wherein "mother" has not entirely disappeared,
but expresses adequation in the "male" figure of Tom, Eva, St. Clare,
and Uncle Tom are snared by the treacheries of an unspoken and
deflected seduction.

We might say that the "seal of heaven" *is* upon Little Eva, if we read
it as the "mark and the knowledge." But beneath "heaven," the
"sacred" intrudes, the "seal," or the "mark" of the "sacred," as the latter
itself marks a conjunction of ambivalence—a culture content at once
"maleficent and beneficent."[41] When, on two distinct occasions,
Ophelia is repelled at the sight of Eva's embracing two "black" figures,
we recognize that her behavior accords perfectly well with a culturally
dictated fear of *contamination*. We need not seek reasons for Ophelia's
scorn in anything that we would remotely call "reasonable," explicit,
or immediately open to the understanding, even if the behavior does
strike us as systematic and obsessional beyond the idiosyncratic markings of character. But it seems certain that the semantic traces into

which "Uncle Tom" is structured—"that far off mystic land of gold, and gems, and spices, and waving palms, and wondrous flowers, and miraculous fertility" (p. 197)—equate "The Negro" not only with "otherness," but with the *matrix* of difference and contradiction that enables this writing. Stowe *needs* "Uncle Tom," along with the novel's considerable display of massive *inarticulations* (the Topsies; the black young, piled in a corner of Uncle Tom's Cabin in a confused heap of noise and motion) in order to *signify* at all, in order, perhaps, to achieve the division in which meaning arises. But distancing herself from her object, the author invests "Little Eva" with the desire to touch, to embrace, the forbidden, concealed like a serpent beneath a bank of flowers.

The renunciation of desire that Gillian Brown argues as the central dynamic of Stowe's "feminine nurture" occurs here under the sign of an indirection as subtle in its appearance as the displaced sexual economies that demarcate Little Eva's connection with both St. Clare and Uncle Tom—and even subtler *because* the line is *written*? In fact, there is no other sentence like this one in this entire novel of so impressive a scope, and, in a female mouth, perhaps no other like it anywhere in American fiction. Because the sentence belongs to a child actant and is contrived in "innocence" and seeming ingenuousness, we are meant to glide right past it with the same kind of tenderhearted admiration that we bring to the sight of a child dangled on its parent's knee, or embracing a pet larger than itself, but we look again. Haley, in the act of expatiating on Tom's virtues to potential buyers aboard the *Belle Rivière*, senses that St. Clare's pretended indifference is just that—pretending—and, indeed, St. Clare, in his fully urbane sophistication and decided amusement at Haley's relative clownishness, goes along with the "show." Misreading St. Clare's gestures, however, Eva softly implores her father to buy Uncle Tom, "putting her arm around [St. Clare's] neck" (p. 166). And then, to my mind, an astonishing sequence of lines is spoken in the aftermath:

"You have money enough, I know. *I want him.*" (P. 166, emphasis mine)

The striking simplicity of "I want him," so unlike the perfectly complicated and elaborate speech of Eva on other fictional occasions, does not invite gloss, except what does it mean, and in particular nearness to money? Are we to suppose that out of the mouth of this babe tumble the words that have not only been denied other females in this text, but, when hinted, very often accomplish very little? Tom and Eliza, for different reasons, are dispatched, in spite of what Emily Shelby and Aunt Chloe *want*. Across the writing, black female figures are bereft of their children, regardless of their tearful and profound *wanting* to keep them; Cassy and Emmeline do not *want* the hideously contrived sexual attentions of Simon Legree foisted upon them, but none of that matters. Are such words threatening in an adult female's discourse, but palatable in the speech of the prepubescent female child?

It seems to me that Stowe dispatches the child to do a woman's job and that by doing so, she not only spares the female for polite readers, who wanted women but not sex, a "vexing genteel dilemma" in Leslie Fiedler's view.[42] But we have hold, it seems, of what becomes, in the course of things in the United States, so scandalous an admission for Anglo-American women to make that it describes a site of marginality. "Desire" in *any form* for the female must be silenced, cut out, banished, "killed" off, and in particular with reference to African male sexuality, here rendered "harmless" under the auspices of a Christian and "civilizing" "mission." I am not content to believe that we must read this novel *just* "sentimentally," and not try it "analytically," as we infer from, say, Fiedler's early reading of *Uncle Tom's Cabin*;[43] I would say that in "sentimental fiction," a term like "slavery" represents partial shorthand and mystification so that we have only *commenced* a reading by invoking it, with much work lying ahead.

Given, then, the complicated discursive and descriptive apparatus from which Stowe's "*Little* Eva" arises, soars, disappears, I would not hesitate to conjecture that the female child figure—in her daring and impermissible *desire*—stands in here for the symptoms of a disturbed female sexuality that American women of Stowe's era could neither articulate nor cancel, only loudly proclaim in the ornamental language, which counterfeits the "sacrificial," of disguise and substitution. Eva could well embody the "Christ-like," but the "Christ-like" in its overlap with the sacrificial figure that René Girard describes—the *expendable* item of culture whose dying will not release the dynamics of a violent reprisal.[44] That Stowe literally "uses" the female child offers no reason at all for a valorization of the gesture as the leading term of a new and different cultural synthesis. We have seen this before—the *sacrificed* girl-child—and in its wake, all heaven and hell break loose, as well they might, if we "learn" anything from the mythical figures of Iphigenia and Clytemnestra. But Stowe's culture—its hateful fathers—has dictated her an *obedient* maternity, alongside the outraged one of Afro-American mothers, which punishes its daughters—as the fathers will do—for the embodiment of its own interdicted desire.

Exactly how "desire"—in whatever way we finally decide to read Little Eva's *wanting*—comes to rest on Tom is not at all clear. Once we can posit a plausibility, which will reside in society's relationships of power, we can determine more precisely what forces have converged in the making of a dyadic taboo—what the shorthand of myth popularly calls, apparently all over "the West" or wherever contact between Africans and their descendants and Europeans and their descendants has been sustained—the "black man" and the "white woman." Because this prohibition was already vividly in place for Stowe's generation of readers, the relationship between the prepubescent "white" female and the adult "black" male is shrouded from the start by a past history. In any case, it seems that Little Eva, in her manifest adumbration of female sexuality and its overlap with the realm of "ubertas," matches the "nature" that attached to Tom so precisely that the impuberty implied between the two figures becomes the sole factor in impeding an explosion of culture's "order" and "degree."

To regard Uncle Tom, therefore, with the innocuousness that the avuncular is meant to suggest would again ignore, or slide over, certain signals that are sporadically thrown in Tom's discursive path. He is not only semiliterate, "having learned late in life" (p. 160), and showing symptoms of dyslexia that Reed will invert to advantage, but he is all the more ripe, consequently, for the signs of a sly watchfulness that would harass any unitary response to this configuration of character. Having been captivated by the stunning "golden head and deep blue eyes [that] peered out upon him from behind some cotton-bale" (p. 162), Tom, in his attraction to Eva, reminds us of the story that is legendarily reported of Pope Gregory's response to the "fair-headed boys" about to be sold into Roman slavery.[45] By virtue of a metathetic error, "Angle" and "Angel" are the same word, as Tom "half believed that he saw one of the angels stepped out of his new testament" (p. 162). Since Tom cannot quite read or "see" the New, or Old, Testament on his own terms, we know that the tracks through which he is reading the "golden" girl as angelic have been planted in him by other eyes. At any rate, Tom is *not* himself an *angel*, and the reasons for this incapacity do not rely on his "darkness" alone.

Actually too shrewd for "innocence," we are coached into believing, Tom, the artful, like a man bent on courtship, has watched

> the little lady a great deal. He knew an abundance of simple acts to pro-
> pitiate and invite the approaches of the little people, and he resolved to
> play his part right skillfully. He could cut cunning little baskets out of
> cherry-stone, could make grotesque faces on hickory-nuts, or odd-jumping
> figures out of elder-pith, and he was a very Pan in the manufacture of
> whistles of all sizes and sorts. His pockets were full of miscellaneous arti-
> cles of attraction, which he hoarded in days of old for his master's chil-
> dren, and which he now produced, with commendable prudence and
> economy, one by one, as overtures for acquaintance and friendship. (Pp.
> 162–63)

A captive person with his pockets full of toys strikes a perfectly ludicrous image to my mind, as it constitutes the sort of inadvertence that a satirist like Reed is bound to exploit, but if the seductive reso-nance of "Pan," "cunning," the "pockets," is allowed to do its work, then we come to regard aspects of this persona—"sweet-tempered," Bible-toting, *Uncle* Tom—as a potentially "dirty old man," "under wraps."

In fact, Tom must remain under cover, in the dark. Doing so, he not only satisfies his culture's, this fiction's, need to estrange his sexu-ality by rendering it "exotic" and unspeakable, but he rewards his observer's fear that he has "one." Negation becomes here an alterna-tive route to confirmation.

Exactly what Stowe had in mind when she canceled the original subtitle of her novel—"the man that was a thing"—is not immediately clear, or, rather, does not offer a clear singularity of impression. Is "thing" in Tom his situation as "an object of desire" for an "essential consciousness"? Is "thinghood" the interpolation of African personality on a horizontal grid that transects a vertical—the "Great Chain of Being"? In other words, is it that juncture at which "mules and men"[46] are situated in a concatenation of differing and contiguous arrangements, as items in Borges's "Chinese Encyclopedia"?[47] At that astonishing juncture of living beings in general, "human" obtains to a status that is both extraordinary, or *more* than human, and under par, *less* than human. But one of the strategies that *Flight to Canada* assumes in the subversion of ontological categories becomes the holding in abeyance of the distance that falls between the writer and his or her "object of desire"—the writing.

The story that is told in Reed's 1976 work is filtered through the fictive consciousness of Reed's poet—Raven Quickskill[48]—who has been commissioned to create the narrative of Uncle Robin. Quickskill's poem, "Flight to Canada," which also provides the novel's epigram, brings celebrity to the poet in a double sense: he is not only a noted author now, anthologized in *The Anthology of Ten Slaves*, but he has been placed on fugitive notice by his master, Arthur Swille III of the ancestral home at Swine'rd, Virginia, from which place Quickskill has successfully escaped to a Great Lakes neighborhood in the vicinity of Buffalo, New York, and William Wells Brown. Confronted with an "order of repossession" brought to him by the "Nebraska Tracers" (pp. 72-73), Quickskill escapes again, together with a former lover, Princess Quaw Quaw Tralaralara, in eventual "flight to Canada." Finding the new place a disappointment to his deepest expectations, Quickskill returns to the Swille Castle after discovering that his former master has been consumed in fire, literally *pushed* into it by the "Etheric Double" of his dead sister Vivian.

But to rehearse the plot of *Flight to Canada* is ultimately dissatisfying itself because the novel does not actually "concern" the plot very much at all. A clever juxtaposition of prior texts, plots, landscapes, icons, historical and other "invented" identities, poems, songs, puns, and sight gags, in a dizzying shift of time and textual perspective, Reed's work is closer in spirit and technique to an evening of American television. In actuality, it is a *media* event. As one of Reed's critics, Jerry H. Bryant, observes, Reed's "context is the American pop culture" the political cartoon, the routine of a stand-up comedian, the high jinks of Mad Comics. His vocabulary and allusions come from the clichés of t.v., best-selling books, newspaper and magazine commercials, and movies."[49] In fact, James R. Lindroth draws a direct connection between *Yellow Back Radio Broke-Down*, one of Reed's first novels, and George Herriman's celebrated cartoon series "Krazy Kat."[50] Unlike traditional writing, *Flight to Canada* so intrudes on the *linearity* of syntagmatic movement that Reed and Stowe cannot be said to share any of the same subject/aesthetic object, to say nothing of the same language. It is doubtful, too, that *Flight to Canada* "is about" "discourse," but it most certainly invades the discursive and its properties in order to blast our own habits of language and the configurations of value and belief that arise in them.

The black reader's long-standing quarrel with *Uncle Tom's Cabin* has to do precisely with Stowe's *arrangement* of lexical items. One might use the same "props," or sequence of "props," and derive an altogether different protocol of reading. *Flight to Canada* demonstrates a writing of insurgence as a matter of systematic interest, but no necessary chumminess obtains between Reed and a putative community of Afro-American readers because of it. In fact, I would go so far as to say that *this* interpretive community becomes one of the *targets* and *topics* of reading, as the overthrow of "slavery" as *the* privileged text of Afro-American historical movement is tried. There are more examples of iconoclastic reinvention in Reed's work than there is time to explore, but one of the most brilliantly concentrated articulations of it occurs when Quickskill, in escape from his button-down pursuers, who are students at a "progressive" school in Nebraska, seeks refuge in the "Slave Hole Café" of "Emancipation City" (pp. 77–81). The entire opening paragraph of the passage should be quoted:

The Slave Hole Café is where the "community" in Emancipation City hangs out. The wallpaper shows a map of the heavens. Prominent is the North Star. A slave with rucksack is pointing it out to his dog. The Café is furnished with tables, chairs, sofas, from different periods. There are quite a few captain's chairs, deacon's benches. There are posters and paintings and framed programs: *Our American Cousin*, a play by Tom Tyler; a photo of Lincoln boarding a train on the way back to Washington from a trip to Emancipation. Sawdust on the floor. A barrel of dill pickles. Above the long bar is a sign PABST BLUE RIBBON. Corn-row and nappy-haired field slaves are here as well as a quadroon or two. Carpetbaggers, Abolitionists. Secessionists, or "Seceshes," as they are called, even some copperheads. The secret society known as the "Rattlesnake" order meets here. They advertise their meetings in the Emancipation newspaper: Attention, Rattlesnakes, come out of your holes . . . by order of President Grand Rattle. Poison Fang, Secretary. (P. 77)

The entire passage works as a self-consciously stylistic manipulation of signs that re-encodes particular graphic units to yield a radically different reading from a more conventional one. On the pronunciation of "café," which, in certain speaking communities, is "unFrenchified," partially depends the "meaning" of the passage. Both "café " and "cáf-e" are simultaneously possible in the hearing since what "happens," graphically, in the passage could occur in both—the captain's chairs" and the "deacon's benches"—but the narrator does not only mean to signal kinds of period pieces of English and American furniture, but to echo in the repertoire of possibilities what a "deacon's bench," or a "captain's chair," might have been in the first place. In black Baptist churches, in parts of the southern United States, at least, there actually is a pew, or set of them, reserved for the clerical functions of "deacons" and "mothers." The referent also sustains this particular resonance. But I am particularly interested in the way that Reed exploits what seems a lost, or muted, "original" sense that reduces or raises the material object to a commercial status. When I buy, say, a "parson's table," or an art deco replication of the lamps that grace the coaches of the Orient Express, the ritual of exchange so covers these duplicated, mass-produced items that their possible historical content, or ritual/aesthetic function, loses any direct significance for me. They exist as "beautiful" objects that are buyable. In the passage, these items constitute units of information that share the same grid of textures and surfaces with signs as disparately tactile and optic as "sawdust" and theater posters. In fact, this "democracy" of "sign-vehicles" is stunning for what adheres and converges—the variety of disjunctive properties "reduced" on a single ground—but, also more importantly, for their self-referentiality *as* sign.

The "Slave Hole Café" and the figurae of its wallpaper offer a demonstrative reading on "iconism and convention,"[51] as Eco outlines this process of relations in *Theory of Semiotics*. It seems to me that a great deal of our current anxiety concerning the projection of a "positive black image," for example, stems in part from the knotty problems that converge on the relationship between an actual experience, or sequences of experiential actualities, and perceptual and graphic content that would translate them. Further, it appears that one's "membership" in the "community" and "loyalty" to it become impugnable, certainly questionable, on the basis of some distant, putative radiance that the black person is imagined to revivify.[52] I recognize, too, that much of the internal debate concerning the status of works like *Uncle Tom's Cabin*, for instance, and, closer to mind, Alice Walker's novel-become-film, *The Color Purple*, might be related to this general program of crises. While this is not the occasion to try to unravel the threads of this massive entanglement, I do think that a studied application of semiological strategies would help reveal the "image crisis" as fundamentally fictive. By that I do not mean to suggest that these "fictions" are inefficacious; as we know, they are *deadly* and *deadening*, having, quite often, the severest political import. I mean, rather, that the ground upon which we invent and reinvent those yoked repetitions that converge on the enterprise of human culture enables the play between "convention" and its possible *translations*.

The "slave hole" was real enough, given everything we already know (or think we do) about the Atlantic slave trade. A male captive with a rucksack on his back, pointing out the North Star to his dog, acquires less certain historical status, although the *conditions* that would constitute such an image are as real as the conditions in which the infamous slave galley appears. We have seen visual representations of both instances, and both tend toward an abstraction of a natural historical/experiential sequence. But there is a difference: whereas "Slave Hole Café" has behind it the numerous descriptions and depictions of "The Brooke Plan," for example, with its representational figurae etched into the drawing, which has behind it, in turn, the plangent "facts of life" that comprise the New World drama of African bodies in passage—their theft and confusion; the actual alteration of human tissue and the blood—the fugitive with a rucksack "imitates" a *possibility*, since "no one" was there to "imagine" the runaway gesture, although the icon of the fugitive is a very popular graphic feature of the historiographies of the period. But I was led to question my own certainty about the status of the image from quite similar passages in Reed and Stowe. In fact, Reed's translation of the fugitive icon strikes an analogy with a scene from *Uncle Tom's Cabin*. Mary Byrd, in trying to arouse the senator's doubts about his own political position on the Fugitive Slave Law, appears to speak in this passage through the narrative device: "He was as bold as a lion about it, and 'mightily convinced' not only himself, but everybody that heard him;—but then his idea of a fugitive was only an idea of the letters that spell the word,—or, at most, the image of a little newspaper picture of a man with a stick and bundle, with 'Ran away from the subscriber' under it." The senator has missed "the real presence of distress" (p. 102).

In one instance, it seems that we can track the image back to a *point of density*—the hole of the slave galley—and in the other, a *potentiality* induced from a *dispersion* of gestures; the image in the writing seems to resolve exactly that way—a rucksack, the heavens, the North Star, a dog. "That a certain image," Eco contends, "is similar to something else does not eliminate the fact that similarity is also a matter of cultural convention."[53] The fugitive icon in Reed's work seems adopted to the end of exposing "convention" as it is deployed through various "masks of repetition." This is indeed the subject of the passage. From newsprint to wallpaper shifts the materiality of the "scene," thus, its "message," or more precisely, the way the receiver feels about the "message." An "iconic solution" may not be inaugurated as a convention, "but it becomes so, step by step, the more its addressee becomes acquainted with it."[54] When an "iconic solution" "fixes" on an object, or subject-position, as it were, it engenders what Eco calls a "perceptual cramp," in which case, as Oscar Wilde reminds us in "The Decay of Lying," the representation "comes to be more true than the real experience."[55] A writer's choice of epistemic weapons, of a "poetics," is as dependent on categories of conventional alignment as the graphic artist's. In both cases, and in specific reference to Stowe and Reed, the semantic and iconic folds in which a discourse on "slavery" embeds situate in "unconventionalized properties," which Eco defines as those that depend "on iconographic convention [and semantic] which has catachresized the previous creative rendering of an actual perceptual experience."[56]

The passage proceeds, then, through a series of "iconic codes" that "establish either a correlation between a graphic sign-vehicle and already coded perceptual unit [as in the instance of the fugitive icon], or between a pertinent unit of the graphic sign-system and a pertinent unit of a semantic system depending on a previous codification of perceptual experience,"[57] as in the image of the "hole" in "Slave Hole Café." But in the final instance, the appropriation of semantic and iconic convention, as common and expected a procedure as it is, compels the attention less for itself than for the outcome it might achieve. Unless fiction can generate, analogous to fields of culture theory, new propositions, or *movement* out of the "perceptual cramp," then we would have neither the possibility of convention, nor *arrest* from it. Reed wants to *change the topic* and the strategies that determine it: We can, "in fact," construct and reconstruct repertoires of usage out of the most painful human/historical experience. So far as I am concerned, the move is a radical one because it insists that (1) "experience" opens itself to the interpretive and narrative act and (2), more important, the initiative to *enunciate*, to attempt a reconstruction of the politics of enunciation—who may speak, under what conditions, and how such speaking has been enabled—determines the fundamental warfare, sometimes euphemized as "culture." With *Flight to Canada*, a fictionalized "slavery" is conduced toward a different *authoring/authority* and a radically determined set of conditions.

Reed's ambitious program might be emblematized in aspects of the name of one of his leading figures—the "Loop Garoo Kid" of *Yellow Back Radio Broke-Down*. Peter Nazareth provides a fascinating gloss on "loop": It "is a sharp bend in a mountain road which almost comes back on itself like a snake. . . . In physics, a loop is an antinode, the node being the point, the line, or surface of a vibrating object free from vibration. To knock for a loop is to throw into confusion. And a loop antenna is used in direction finding equipment and in radio receivers. Once you get to the multiple meanings, you, the reader, begin to loop."[58] In all these suggestions, coiling, recoiling, and rotation upon rotation are implied, as even the radio receiver must be open to impressions, all around, in order to do its work. To say that "Reed wants us to short-circuit the whole mess, to break it down,"[59] and I would add, rope it in and tie it up, renders a fairly precise notion of reading Reed as process.

Even though *Flight to Canada feels* like a huge, occasionally striking mural that one might *visit*, compared to Stowe's encyclopedic elaborations that hold us—for days—to the reader's "hot seat," Reed's work actually takes as much "real" reading time as Stowe's precisely because a century and a half have gone by in the American aftermath of *Uncle Tom's Cabin*. The narrative device of *Flight to Canada* traverses a complicated repertoire of textual reference that "loops" in sources as disparate in context as Tennyson's "Idylls of the King," Poe's "Fall of the House of Usher," histories of American Reconstruction, and apocrypha and gossip concerning Abraham and Mrs. Lincoln, Jefferson and Varina Davis. But Reed also pays a great deal of attention to the "fine print," or the kind of detail that we associate with footnotes and passages in asterisks; for instance, the "copperheads" of the passage I cited demarcate historical content as well as an associative device. In propinquity to the secret society of the "Order of the Rattlesnakes," a "copperhead" is related to the rattlesnake, but does not rattle. The notion of a perniciousness that does not announce itself accords well with the "Copperhead" in "culture"—the proslavery labor movement, focused in the North, that was enabled, according to Du Bois, "to turn the just indignation of the workers against the Negro laborers, rather than against the capitalists."[60] In other words, there are snakes hanging out at the "Slave Hole" in "secret" meeting and "liberal" clothing. The sweep of syncretisms provides here one kind of content; the exploitation of the frozen, reified signification—which we immediately recognize as such—presents another, for example, the "military man," Lincoln's "aide," the "Mammy" of the Swille estate, "Ms. Swille," the "quadroon," and the like. For every single page of the 192 printed pages of the edition I am using, there could be as many source pages to read as the novel is long. This multiplying of textual allusiveness and the freedom of movement that is granted the spatiotemporal economies of the work would suggest that "narrative time" for Reed is not imagined as a linear progression alone. It "imitates" the tricks and intricacies of the loop.

Flight to Canada, relatedly, manipulates narrative time as an "eternal present." In that regard, the past is subject to change,[61] as certain well-known historical episodes are reinvented here in contemporary perspective: The assassination of the novel's "Abe Lincoln" is televised, just as Arthur Swille III is translated into a slaveholding multinational corporate head, or, in the words of the character of Lincoln, "a swell titanic titan of ten continents" (p. 38). Swille's estate, called "Camelot," is equipped with telephones and sophisticated electronic devices; Stray Leechfield's carriage [features] "factory climate-control air conditioning, vinyl top, AM/FM stereo radio, full leather interior, power lock doors, six-way power seat, power windows, white-wall wheels, door-edge guards, bumper impact strips, rear defroster and soft-ray glass" (p. 46). Reed's stunning anachronisms resituate variously precise portions of cultural content so that we gain a different "cartography" of historicized fiction. These radical displacements sever *event* from a desiccated spatial focus so that it comes to belong once again to the realm of *possibility*, the possibility of *movement*. The interlardings of reference do not only yield what we currently call a "writerly text," or a *plural* text, but a plurality bent on showing its seams. In other words, artifice, "show," ingenuity, announce themselves as such.

The outcome does not yield a particularly "beautiful" work, nor a work that enamors us to, or engages us with, this writing as process entirely. We are also coerced to change our mind about *who* and *what* "character" is. The discussion that Todorov offers seems to capture *Flight to Canada* as an exemplary instance: "The character is the subject of the narrative proposition. As such he is reduced to a pure syntactic function, without any semantic content. The attributes, as well as the actions, play the role of predicate in a proposition and are only provisionally linked to a subject. It will be convenient to identify this subject by a proper name that incarnates him in most cases, insofar as the name identifies a spatio-temporal unity without describing its properties."[62] Even though we can say, I think, with a great deal of justification that Reed's "characters" fit, more or less, this discomforting, unromanticized, demystified subject, we must also hold open the possibility that both the reader's and writer's *investment* in these modes of proposition keeps the "character" alive in the old way.

Because our energies are *always* engaged by the ontological dimension of "character," although we are urged, these days, to "bracket" such concern, or suspend it, or cut it out altogether, we infuse "character" with subjective properties. Reed's "Uncle Robin," for example, may be considered a revisionary proposition, since he names a character that appears in the catalog of proslavery fictional responses to *Uncle Tom's Cabin*. According to Richard Yarborough, a novel by John H. Page was published in 1853, a year following *Uncle Tom's Cabin*, in which Page supposedly intended to present the *southern* view of the "peculiar institution." Page entitled his work *Uncle Robin in His Cabin in Virginia and Tom without One in Boston*.[63] A semantic marker called "Uncle Robin" appears in *Flight to Canada*, and "he" lives in the "Frederick Douglass Houses" of Swille's "Virginia." But *this* Uncle Robin proposes so significant a blow to the power relations of dominance and enslavement that we lose entirely any allegiance to a strictly semiologic configuration of "character." In fact, we could say that Uncle Robin, in the manipulation of signs, changes the letter, which insurgent act makes the world a different place.

When the relatives and the "property" of Arthur Swille III gather for a reading of his will, following his bizarre death, nothing is revealed by its provisions that we have not expected, given what we know already about "Mammy Barracuda," "Cato, the Graffado," and the rest. But we suspect that a loop in the action—a curve turning back on itself in the road—has been prepared when the officiating magistrate's mouth opens wide and he begins to "stutter and rattle the paper in his trembling hands" as he reads, "'And to Uncle Robin, I leave this Castle, these hills and everything behind the gates of the Swille Virginia estate.' Much commotion" (p. 180). We miss the isochrony in "gates" and "estate," even though syllabic symmetry elsewhere in the novel has served a parodic function, because the joke is Uncle Robin's. We concentrate on what becomes as incredible a stroke of the accidental for the reader as it is for the judge. Swille's guilt, however, has not compelled him, we later learn, to an act of unimpeachable magnanimity; rather, Uncle Robin has "dabbled with the will" (p. 183). "I prayed to one of our gods, and he came to me in a dream. He was wearing a top hat, raggedy britches and an old black opera waistcoat. He had on alligator shoes. He was wearing the top hat, too, and was puffing on a cigar. Look like Lincoln's hat. That Stovepipe. He said it was okay to do it. The 'others' had approved" (p. 183). Even if a visual pun on "Lincoln" appears in Uncle Robin's dream, overlapping, unmistakably, with "one of our gods," we recognize the auspiciousness of Uncle Robin's plan. It turns out that "Swille had something called *dyslexia*. Words came to him scrambled and jumbled. I became his reading and writing. Like a computer, only this computer left itself Swille's whole estate. Property joining forces with property. I left me his whole estate. I'm it, too. Me and it got more it" (p. 184; emphasis mine).

The reader will recall that Uncle Tom is Stowe's dyslexic man, revealed in young George Shelby's instructing him in the mysteries of "g" and "q," as "Uncle Tom laboriously brought up the tail of his 'g' the wrong side out" (p. 32). Given the propositions that Todorov contends make up "character," *this* "character" capitulates to the closure of mystery. "G" and "q" are easily confused in the abecedarian stages of our apprenticeship in language learning and, beyond that, in the routine play of letters that "confuse" the adult reading, or refuse to stay put, to mean *how* we want. Typewriters and computers have been known to make very similar errors of transposition. But it seems to me that Uncle Robin, in celebrating the sheer malice of an arbitrary materiality, succeeds in cracking the code of meaning, which, for Reed, relies on a riddle: if you change the joke, you slip the yoke.[64]

NOTES

1. Harriet Beecher Stowe, *Uncle Tom's Cabin, with an Afterword by John William Ward* (New York: New American Library, 1966), 179–80. (All direct quotations from the novel come from this source, hereafter cited parenthetically in the text.)

2. Harriet Beecher Stowe, *The Key to Uncle Tom's Cabin, Presenting the Original Facts and Documents upon Which the Story is Founded Together with Corroborative Statements Verifying the Truth of the Work.* (London: Clark, Beeton, and Co., Foreign Booksellers, n.d), 45.

3. Ibid., 46.

4. Ibid., 46.

5. Ibid., 46.

6. Nancy C. M. Hartsock, *Money, Sex, and Power: Toward a Feminist Historical Materialism* (New York: Longmans, 1983), 192.

7. Kenneth Burke, *A Grammar of Motives* (New York: Prentice-Hall, 1952), 122.

8. Gillian Brown, "Getting in the Kitchen with Dinah: Domestic Politics in *Uncle Tom's Cabin,*" *American Quarterly* 36, no. 4 (1984), 505.

9. My notion of an intertextual eventuality between these texts is heavily influenced by Michel Foucault's *Archaeology of Knowledge and the Discourse on Language*, trans. A. M. Sheridan Smith (New York: Harper Colophon Books, 1972), 193.

10. Richard Yarborough, "Strategies of Black Characterization in *Uncle Tom's Cabin* and the Early Afro-American Novel," in *New Essays on Uncle*

Tom's Cabin, ed. Eric J. Sundquist, Jr. (New York: Cambridge University Press, 1986), 45–85, 68.

11. George Eliot, "Review of *Dred; A Tale of the Great Dismal Swamp,*" in *Critical Essays on Harriet Beecher Stowe*, ed. Elizabeth Ammons (Boston: G. K. Hall and Co., 1980), 43.

12. Yarborough, "Strategies of Black Characterization," 63.

13. Foucault, *Archaeology of Knowledge*, 58.

14. Ishmael Reed, *Flight to Canada* (New York: Avon books, 1976), 29. (All direct quotations from the novel come from this source, hereafter cited parenthetically in the text.)

15. Umberto Eco, *A Theory of Semiotics* (Bloomington: Indiana University Press, 1979), 215.

16. Ibid., 81.

17. Stephen Greenblatt's impressive formulation of "improvisational skills" concerning Shakespeare's Iago richly informs my own thinking about intertextual possibilities between *Uncle Tom's Cabin* and *Flight to Canada*: "I shall call that mode *improvisation*, by which I mean the ability both to capitalize on the unforeseen and to transform given materials into one's own scenario" (*Renaissance Self-Fashioning: From More to Shakespeare* [Chicago: University of Chicago Press, 1980], 227).

18. Eco, *A Theory of Semiotics*, 66.

19. I refer here not very precisely to René Girard's formulation of the triangle of desire in *Deceit, Desire, and the Novel: Self and Other in Literary Structure*, trans. Yvonne Frecerro (Baltimore: Johns Hopkins University Press, 1965), 1–52. There is, of course, no obvious "rivalry" for Eva's affections between Uncle Tom and Augustine St. Clare, but imagining for the moment that these central figures embody wider psychocultural functions, we might say that "Little Eva" is made to represent, indeed, the gynophobic object of desire, dangerously poised between the "black" male and his freedom, essentially "held in fief" by the "white" male.

20. Ann Douglass, *The Feminization of American Culture* (New York: Alfred A. Knopf, 1977), 3–13.

21. Jane Tompkins, *Sensational Designs* (New York: Oxford University Press, 1985), 124–25. One of the most recent definitive texts on American women writers, Tompkins's work offers a brilliant paradigm of conceptualiza-

tion on the issues. Although I accept her basic premises, my most significant reservations about this work have to do with the muting of "race" in this cultural analysis.

22. Ibid., 125.

23. Ibid., 126, emphasis Tompkins's.

24. Ibid., 126, emphasis mine.

25. Elizabeth Ammons, "Heroines in *Uncle Tom's Cabin*," *American Literature* 49 (May 1977): 161–79.

26. James Baldwin, *Notes of a Native Son* (New York: Bantam Books, 1972), 13.

27. Even though one could draw on a number of sermons from black preaching tradition that subvert the discursive economies of sacrifice, I refer specifically to the Washington, D.C. pulpit of Francis Grimke, whose sermons, speeches, and letters have been edited by Carter G. Woodson: *Works of Francis James Grimke*, 4 vols. (Washington, D.C.: Associated Publishers, 1942).

28. Kenneth Burke, *The Rhetoric of Religion: Studies in Logology* (Berkeley and Los Angeles: University of California Press, 1970), 14–15.

29. Brown, "Getting in the Kitchen with Dinah," 518.

30. Sundquist, Introduction to *New Essays on Uncle Tom's Cabin*, 35.

31. Catherine Beecher, *Treatise on Domestic Economy* (reprint; New York: Schocken Books, 1977).

32. Karen Halttunen, "Gothic Imagination and Social Reform: The Haunted Houses of Lyman Beecher, Henry Ward Beecher, and Harriet Beecher Stowe," *New Essays on Uncle Tom's Cabin*, 110.

33. Ibid., 114.

34. Ibid., 119.

35. Ibid., 119, emphasis mine.

36. Ammons, "Heroines in *Uncle Tom's Cabin*," 164.

37. Sundquist, Introduction to *New Essays on Uncle Tom's Cabin*, 35.

38. Ibid.

39. Tompkins, *Sensational Designs*, 137.

40. Halttunen, "Gothic Imagination," 115.

41. René Girard, *Violence and the Sacred*, trans. Patrick Gregory (Baltimore: Johns Hopkins University Press, 1977), 257.

42. Leslie Fiedler, "Harriet Beecher Stowe's Novel of Sentimental Protest," in *Critical Essays on Harriet Beecher Stowe*, 114.

43. Ibid., 115. Fiedler provides a more recent assessment of Stowe's work in "The Many Mothers of *Uncle Tom's Cabin*," in his *What Was Literature? Class Culture and Mass Society* (New York: Simon and Schuster, 1982).

44. The dynamics of the mechanism of violent reprisal are formulated in Girard's *Violence and the Sacred*.

45. This narrative is reported in Albert C. Baugh's *History of the English Language*, 2d ed. (New York: Appleton-Century-Crofts, 1957), 94.

46. I borrow this formulation from Zora Neale Hurston's celebrated ethnographic study, *Mules and Men: Negro Folktales and Voodoo Practices in the South* (New York: Harper and Row, 1970).

47. Michel Foucault, *The Order of Things: An Archaeology of the Human Sciences* (New York: Vintage Books, 1973), xv.

48. Joe Weixlmann provides interesting speculation on the origins of Raven Quickskill's name from the raven myth of the Tlingit community of Native Americans in "Ishmael Reed's Raven," *The Review of Contemporary Fiction* 4, no. 2 (Summer 1984): 205.

49. Jerry H. Bryant, "Old Gods and New Demons: Ishmael Reed and His Fiction," *Review of Contemporary Fiction* 4, no. 2 (Summer 1984): 196.

50. James R. Lindroth, "From Krazy Kat to Hoodoo: Aesthetic Discourse in the Fiction of Ishmael Reed," *Review of Contemporary Fiction* 4, no. 2 (Summer 1984): 227.

51. Eco, *A Theory of Semiotics*, 204–205.

52. The destructive effects of the mythologizing of Afro-American personality are powerfully articulated in Deborah E. McDowell's "Boundaries: Or Distant Relations and Close Kin," proceedings from the Symposium in Afro-American Literature, convened by Houston Baker at the American College, Bryn Mawr, Pa., April 1987.

53. Eco, *A Theory of Semiotics*, 204.

54. Ibid., 205.

55. Ibid., 205.

56. Ibid., 207.

57. Ibid., 208.

58. Peter Nazareth, "Heading Them Off at the Pass: The Fiction Of Ish-

mael Reed," *Review of Contemporary Fiction* 4, no. 2 (Summer 1984): 219.

59. Ibid.

60. W. E. B. Du Bois, *Black Reconstruction in America, 1860–1880* (New York: Meridian Books, 1968), 102–103.

61. Nazareth, "Heading Them Off at the Pass," 211.

62. Oswald Ducrot and Tzvetan Todorov, *Encyclopedic Dictionary of the Sciences of Language*, trans. Catherine Porter (Baltimore: Johns Hopkins University Press, 1979), 222.

63. Yarborough, "Strategies of Black Characterization," 58.

64. The title of my essay offers a riff, of course, on Ralph Ellison's celebrated piece, "Change the Joke and Slip the Yoke," *Shadow and Act* (New York: Signet Books, 1966), 61–74.

 *William L. Andrews*

The Representation of Slavery and the Rise of Afro-American Literary Realism 1865–1920

The most famous metaphor of slavery in the history of Afro-American literature appears in the climax of the *Narrative of the Life of Frederick Douglass, an American Slave*, in which Douglass reconstructs the significance of his struggle with the slave-breaker, Edward Covey, on a hot August morning in 1834. Triumph over Covey, known as "the snake" among his slaves, became Douglass's "glorious resurrection, from the tomb of slavery, to the heaven of freedom."[1] A little more than a half century after Douglass's *Narrative* was published, the most infamous metaphor of slavery in the history of black American literature appeared in the first chapter of Booker T. Washington's *Up from Slavery*. When we "look facts in the face," Washington states, "we must acknowledge that, notwithstanding the cruelty and moral wrong of slavery, the ten million Negroes inhabiting this country, who themselves or whose ancestors went through the school of American slavery, are in a stronger and more hopeful condition, materially, intellectually, morally, and religiously, than is true of an equal number of black people in any other portion of the globe."[2] The disparities between these two metaphors are striking. The antebellum writer says slavery was like a tomb, in which he languished in what Orlando Patterson would call "social death" and from which he was resurrected only by rebellious effort.[3] The postbellum writer, on the other hand, compares slavery to a school, in which he and his fellows received, rather than lost, social purpose and from which they graduated not by violence but by sanctioned behavior like industry and dutifulness. I do not call attention to this difference between Douglass and Washington in order to question the reliability of one or the other as historian of slavery. The metaphorical shift between the two most influential slave narratives in American literature urges a more important inquiry, I believe, into the dynamics of Afro-American literary, rather than sociopolitical, history.

Throughout the nineteenth century and well into the twentieth, autobiographies of former slaves dominated the Afro-American narrative tradition. Approximately sixty-five American slave narratives were published in book or pamphlet form before 1865. Between the Civil War and the onset of the depression, at least fifty more ex-slaves saw their autobiographies in print, to a large extent eclipsing in their own time the influence, if not the memory, of their antebellum predecessors. Yet with the exception of criticism on *Up from Slavery*, there has been little investigation into what I shall call the postbellum slave narrative, nor has there been any serious study of the large number of black autobiographies in the late nineteenth and early twentieth centuries that were written in the shadow of the postbellum slave narrative, especially Washington's.[4] It is imperative to read the slave narrative tradition wholly, however, if we wish to reckon with the significance of the crucial shift in the metaphor of slavery that highlights the Douglass and Washington texts. If we read the Afro-American autobiographical tradition from 1765 to 1920 in toto, we can see that major parameters of this tradition—such as the representation of slavery—underwent revision, not only according to the differing perspectives of individual writers but also in relation to the changing social and political priorities of successive generations of freedmen and freedwomen.

The slave narrative took on its classic form and tone between 1840 and 1860, when the romantic movement in American literature was in its most influential phase. Transcendentalists like Theodore Parker welcomed antebellum slave narratives (and Douglass's in particular) into the highest echelon of American literature, insisting that "all the original romance of Americans is in them, not in the white man's novel."[5] Douglass's celebration of selfhood in his 1845 *Narrative* might easily be read as a black contribution to the literature of romantic individualism and anti-institutionalism. Ten years later Douglass's second autobiography, *My Bondage and My Freedom*, deconstructs his 1845 self-portrait with typical romantic irony. The idea of heroic slaves like Douglass resurrecting themselves from graves of the spirit by forceful resistance to authority undoubtedly appealed to an era fascinated by the romantic agon, the life-and-death contest of the spirit of revision against all that represses it.[6] But after the Civil War, few ex-slave autobiographers recounted their lives in the manner of Douglass. The stunningly different treatments of bondage and selfhood in *Up from Slavery*, for instance, signal a new wave of revisionism in postbellum Afro-American literature, instanced in the reaction of later slave autobiographers to what they perceived as romanticized interpretations of the pre-emancipation past, whether by black or white writers. By the turn of the century, slave narrators viewed slavery and its significance to the advancement of black people in an increasingly pragmatic perspective, delineated most effectively in *Up from Slavery*. This immensely influential slave narrative articulates a quasi-literary realism whose rhetoric, conventions, and cultural import need to be examined if we are to reckon adequately with the effort on the part of turn-of-the-century black novelists to make fiction address matters of fact.

The antebellum slave narrative was the product of fugitive bondmen who rejected the authority of their masters and their socialization as slaves and broke away, often violently, from slavery. Since the slave's right to rebel was a hotly debated issue in the 1840s and 1850s, the classic antebellum slave narrative highlights the brutalizing horrors of slavery in order to justify forcible resistance and escape as the only way a black could preserve his or her humanity. Through an emphasis on slavery as deprivation— buttressed by extensive evidence of a lack of adequate food, clothing, and shelter; the denial of basic familial rights; the enforced ignorance of most religious or moral precepts; and so on—the antebellum narrative pictures the South's "peculiar institution" as a wholesale assault on everything precious to humankind. Under slavery, civilization reverts to a Hobbesian state of nature; if left to its own devices slavery will pervert master and mistress into monsters of cupidity and power-madness and reduce their servant to a nearly helpless object of exploitation and cruelty. Ultimately this objectifying power of slavery is what the antebellum slave narrative protests against most eloquently by demonstrating the evolution of a liberating subjectivity in the slave's life, up to and including the act of writing autobiography itself.

Antebellum slave narrators like Douglass and Henry Bibb[7] trace their salvation back to an intuition of individual uniqueness and a sense of special destiny which they claim has inspired them since their early youth. "The fire of liberty," Bibb states, "seemed to be a part of my nature; it was first revealed to me by the inevitable laws of nature's God."[8] The slave's outward struggle for physical freedom emanates from an inner conflict played out in the arena of his consciousness, where the fire of his Promethean self contends with the "mental and spiritual darkness" (in James Pennington's typical image)[9] of slavery. Ironically, however, the enlightenment provided by the Promethean fire within only reveals the tremendous gulf between the slave's subjective view of himself as a unique essence and slavery's objectified view of him as a thing. As a result of such revelations, the slave's world takes on an absolute, binary character.[10] The only way he can assert his existence as a subject is by rebelling against the system that renders him an object. In the act of rebellion, the slave realizes himself, gives order to the chaos of his condition, and claims what we might call an existential authenticity and freedom while still in bondage.

What the slave rebel seeks in his flight to the North, however, is much more than an existential alternative to the non-being of slavery. The quest is for an ideal of freedom, a condition in which one may liberate the essential self within through expressive action and the power of the word. Few fugitive slaves say that their goal, when they fled the South, was to make a name for themselves as speakers and/or writers in the North. Still, the most memorable antebellum slave narrators treat their arrival on the abolitionist lecture platform or their acceptance of the antislavery pen as the fulfillment of their destiny. Literacy is considered the ultimate form of power in the antebellum slave narrative, for at least two reasons. First, language is assumed to signify the subject and hence to ratify the slave narrator's humanity as well as his authority. Second, white bigotry and fear presumably cannot withstand the onslaught of the truth feelingly represented in the simple personal history of a former slave. This romantic trust in the power of language did not go unchallenged in the antebellum black autobiography, as I have argued in my book *To Tell a Free Story*.[11] Still, given the paucity of alternative weapons for blacks in the antislavery struggle, the idea that the word could make them free remained an article of faith in Afro-American literature of the antebellum era.

The abolition of involuntary servitude in 1865 forced the slave narrator in the postwar era to reevaluate the purpose of his or her prospective literary enterprise. Since ex-slaves no longer needed to denounce slavery to white America, the story of their past no longer carried the same social or moral import. Upon the demise of Reconstruction, however, and the rise of reactionary racism in the New South, many ex-slaves felt a renewed sense of purpose as firsthand commentators on the South before and after the war. The author of the new slave narrative, however, was no longer the rebel-fugitive whose ascent to freedom in the North had been celebrated in romantic fashion in the antebellum era. The large majority of postbellum ex-slave autobiographers—three out of every four, to be more exact—take pride in having endured slavery without having lost their sense of worth or purpose and without having given in to the despair that the antebellum narrator pictures as the lot of so many who languished in slavery.[12] Acknowledging that rare "moral courage" was required to engineer a successful escape from slavery, the typical postbellum narrator insists that slaves who never took such a step could still claim a dignity and heroism of their own. "There were thousands of high-toned and high-spirited slaves," Henry Clay Bruce recalls in his 1895 narrative, "who had as much self-respect as their masters, and who were industrious, reliable and truthful. . . . These slaves knew their own helpless condition" and understood that "they had no rights under the laws of the land." Yet "they did not give up in abject servility, but held up their heads and proceeded to do the next best thing under the circumstances, which was, to so live and act as to win the confidence of their masters, which could only be done by faithful service and an upright life." When these "reliables," as Bruce terms them, were "freed by the war, the traits which they had exhibited for generations to such good effect, were brought into greater activity, and have been largely instrumental in making the record of which we feel so proud to-day."[13]

These remarks from Bruce's autobiography, *The New Man*, exemplify the pragmatism of the postbellum slave narrative in several respects. Bruce implicitly rejects the existential thesis of the antebellum narrative, namely, that because slavery was inimical to a slave's intellectual, moral, and spiritual development, rebellion was necessary to the slave's assertion and preservation of selfhood. Bruce argues that slaves could and did achieve "self-respect" without rebelling or running away to the North. Instead of the "either-or" conditions of the antebellum narrator—either self-affirming rebellion or self-abnegating acceptance of chattelism—Bruce, like most postbellum narrators, stresses that slaves could and did choose "the next best thing" according to relative, rather than absolute, standards of value. There is ample evidence of forcible, as well as passive, resistance to mean-spirited masters in slave narratives like Bruce's, a testimony to the fact that slaves in the postbellum narrative treasure their dignity as much as their counterparts in the antebellum narrative. But in the postbellum narrative, the measure of a slave's dignity is much more pragmatic than existential, more public than private, and more tangible and considerably less ideal than it is in the most famous antebellum narratives. Thus, while Douglass's fight with Covey epitomizes the antebellum ideal of "manhood," a typical postbellum slave narrator like George Henry sets out to prove "that though black I was a man in every sense of the word" by recalling his superlative achievements as a hostler, a ship's captain, even as overseer, in slavery.[14] In the postbellum narrative, a slave does not have to fight back to claim a free man's sense of empowering honor; diligence in his duties and pride in a task well done say as much or more about a black man's respectability as running away, especially if that black man is also a family man.[15] Ultimately, men like Bruce and Henry appeal to the pragmatic test of history to vindicate their sense of honor. The success stories that these "new men" chronicle in their post-emancipation years are

designed to demonstrate that the course they followed as slaves prepared them well to seize opportunity in freedom and turn it to honorable account, both socially and economically.

The pragmatism of the postbellum slave narrator stems primarily
from his willingness to interpret and evaluate slavery according to its
practical consequences in the real world of human action. While the
antebellum narrative did not ignore the practical effects of slavery on
blacks and whites in the South, it rested its antislavery case on religious and ethical absolutes like Bibb's "inevitable laws of Nature's
God," or what William Craft called "the sacred rights of the weak."[16]
The postbellum narrator rarely appeals to such ideals or to the right-
eous indignation that let his antebellum predecessor condemn slavery
so categorically. Instead he asks his reader to judge slavery simply and
dispassionately on the basis of what Booker T. Washington liked to
call "facts," by which the Tuskegean meant something other than empirical data. In *Up from Slavery*, as in many other postbellum slave narratives, a factual evaluation of slavery exploits what William James
would later call the "practical cash-value" of the word, its significance
in the present day.[17] What slavery was in the past is not so important
as what slavery means, or (more importantly) can be construed to
mean, in the present. A factual view of slavery, for Washington, is concerned less with a static concept of historical truth, frozen in the past,
than with the need for rhetorical power in the ever-evolving present.
To the postbellum slave narrator, particularly Washington, slavery
needed to be reviewed and reempowered as a concept capable of effect-
ing change, of making a difference ultimately in what white people
thought of black people as freedmen, not slaves. The facts of slavery
in the postbellum narrative, therefore, are not so much what happened *then*—bad though it was—as what *makes* things, good things,
happen now.

Looking the facts of the present (more than the past) in the face,
Washington could justifiably call slavery a school in which black
Americans had learned much about the necessity of hard work, per-
severance, and self-help as survival skills in their difficult passage in
the antebellum South. The fact of turn-of-the-century American

"scientific" racism, which stereotyped "the Negro" as degraded, ignorant, incompetent, and servile, demanded that slavery be re-presented anew, not as a condition of deprivation and degradation, but as a period of training and testing, from which the slave graduated with high honors and even higher ambitions. Given the changed sociopolitical circumstances, it is not surprising to find the postbellum slave narrator treating slavery more as an economic proving ground than an existential battleground for southern black people. The slave past, if effectively represented, could provide the freedman and freedwoman with credentials that the new industrial-capitalist order might respect. By the turn of the century, blacks were realizing their need for a usable American past on which they could build.[18] They could also see that southern whites needed to be reminded of who had built the Old South and who could help to build a New South as well.[19] The agenda of the postbellum slave narrative thus emphasizes unabashedly the tangible contribution that blacks made to the South, in and after slavery, in order to rehabilitate the image of the freedman, not the idea of slavery, in the eyes of business America.

Although in some ways a typical postbellum slave narrative, *Up from Slavery* stands out today, as always, because of its articulation of an accommodationist strategy that, though by no means original, Washington managed to identify as his own.[20] What we would call accommodationism, however, is what the Tuskegean would have termed realism. What are the sources of real power in the real world? asks the writer of *Up from Slavery*. In the antebellum slave narrative, as I have already noted, the answer is almost unanimous. Knowledge is power, and the fundamental source of knowledge is literacy, the ability to open one's mind to the words of others and to liberate other minds with a text of one's own. As an ex-slave and an educator, Washington pays lip service to the importance of reading in his own life and in the training of his people. But in his preferred persona as pragmatic student of power, he demotes men of the word and elevates men of action to the putative leadership of his people. The irony of the preeminent black speaker and writer of his day identifying himself as a man of real acts, not mere words, should not prevent us from recognizing the literary significance of Washington's antiliterary thesis. *Up from Slavery* is, in its own quiet and indirect—should I say sly?—way, a manifesto of a quasi-literary realism that attempts to restrict the traditional sovereignty of the black wordsmith by chaining the signifier to a preexistent signified and thus making the word merely reflective, rather than constitutive, of reality.

Washington's realism entails a radical distinction between deeds and words. "The actual sight of a first-class house that a Negro has built is ten times more potent than pages of discussion about a house that he ought to build, or perhaps could build" (p. 297). Action, Washington insists, produces things; discussion, by contrast, produces only more discussion. "Instead of studying books so constantly, how I wish that our schools and colleges might learn to study men and things!" (p. 243). The men Washington studies are, of course, white men of action and substance, like Andrew Carnegie, Collis P. Huntington, and William McKinley. In stark contrast with them are black men of words—in particular, southern politicians, preachers, and educators. These men, Washington argues, have too often made speaking and writing a refuge from doing, from working productively for the good of the race. As he surveys the recent history of his people, he finds that politicians stirred up in the people only an "artificial" desire to hold public office; preachers inspired in literate black men only a self-serving "call to preach"; teachers merely pandered to "the craze for Greek and Latin learning" (p. 256) among pathetically ignorant blacks. Instead of doing tangible good, all this preaching and teaching and speech-making created in the minds of rural southern blacks a pernicious notion, namely, that an alternative resource of power existed to what Washington called the "real, solid foundation" (p. 260) of black advancement, the agrarian life. Even Washington had to acknowledge that the black community had traditionally revered the man of the word as "a very superior human being, something bordering almost on the supernatural" (p. 256) in the case of those who understood the mystery of foreign languages. Such men seemed not to require "the solid and never deceptive foundation of Mother Nature" (p. 261), that is, a grounding in the life of "the soil," to exercise power and excite envy among southern blacks.[21] Washington's fear was that the example of Afro-American men of the word would encourage young blacks to believe that the route to black power was not hand-to-mouth, from act to word, but rather just the reverse, from performing word to reforming act. Washington pays inadvertent tribute to these black masters of the speech-act by noting that they "live by their wits" instead of by their hands and that the white South regards them with a perplexed and uneasy suspicion.

Few can read *Up from Slavery* today without recognizing that Washington also lived by his wits and in a consummate manner. A former political stump speaker and student of the ministry, Washington clearly understood the power of the word in the mouth of an artful and ambitious black man. "I never planned to give any large part of my life to speaking in public," he blandly remarks, adding, "I have always had more of an ambition to *do* things than merely to talk *about* doing them" (p. 320). Yet no black man could have built Tuskegee Institute without knowing that action proceeds from speech and that speech is itself a most potent form of action. Washington acknowledges that he authorized the erection of Porter Hall, the first building on the Tuskegee campus, before he had the money to pay for it. He relied on his charm and good name in the community to secure loans to complete the edifice. He had no capital at all when he conceived of putting up a second building, but, as he offhandedly comments, "We decided to give the needed building a name" (p. 309) anyway. Naming the building Alabama Hall proved, of course, a shrewd political maneuver that helped to ensure the continuation of the state funding on which Washington depended so much in the early years. This speech-act alone, so reminiscent of the talismanic power of naming in the slave narrative tradition, belies Washington's insistence that words merely publicize deeds. Thus, even though he claims that he always "had a desire to do something to make the world better, and *then* be able to speak to the world about that thing" (p. 249; emphasis mine), Washington had the wit to see that speaking makes doing possible and that reality is contingent on language, not the other way around.

Nevertheless, in an effort to subvert the "almost supernatural" status of the man of words in the black community, the author of *Up from Slavery* presents himself as a naturalist, arguing that only from a rootedness in "nature" does he derive the "strength for the many duties and hard places that await me" (p. 356) in the real world. Washington is not talking about communing with Nature in some romantic fashion. His need is more immediate and tangible: "I like, as often as possible, to touch nature, not something that is artificial or an imitation, but the real thing" (p. 355). Hence it is no surprise to find Washington depreciating belles-lettres and enthusing over newspapers as "a constant source of delight and recreation." Obviously, fiction, poetry, and drama are artificial and merely imitative of "the real thing." Only one kind of storytelling can satisfy Washington's appetite for realism, namely, "biography," for which he claims "the greatest fondness." Why he should prefer biography to all other kinds of reading is plain enough: "I like to be sure that I am reading about a real man or a real thing" (p. 355). But the way Washington prefaces his predictable desire for the "real thing"—"I like to be *sure*"—suggests that he knows that readers of biography do not always get what they expect or want, nor does biography always assure its readers of their ability to distinguish between the real and the artificial. Maybe this is one reason why Washington is at such pains in writing his own biography to portray himself as a plain and simple man of facts, "the real thing" among autobiographers, a man who represents himself as no more than what he is. Washington *knows* the prejudice in his white audience against black men of words as truth-tellers; this is a major reason why he claims he is a man of acts and facts.[22] By repeatedly declaring his "great faith in the power and influence of facts" and his conviction that one can touch the real thing in biography, Washington acts to shore up the foundation of *Up from Slavery*, which we can see is not so much grounded in real things as in linguistic demonstrations of realism.

Capitalizing on the postbellum slave narrator's pragmatic revision of the facts of slavery, *Up from Slavery* promulgates a concept of realism which challenges the traditional status of the sign in the Afro-American narrative tradition. By claiming a radical distinction between action and speech and by disclaiming language as anything more than a referential medium, Washington denies the performative dimension of representation. The consummate rhetorician, he tries to pass for a realist, we might say, since this lets him keep his agenda masked behind a semblance of nonrhetorical *vraisemblance*. If Washington could define the terms by which realism would be judged in Afro-American writing, then he could consign literary representation to a *re*active status in Afro-American culture, thereby robbing it of the expressive power that the word had held in the black community since the antebellum era. The rise of Tuskegee realism then, foregrounded by the postbellum slave narrative and reinforced by numerous autobiographies of Washington's protégés, imitators, and admirers, discounts the hard-won victory of antebellum narratives like *My Bondage and My Freedom* and *Incidents in the Life of a Slave Girl*, texts that liberated black narrative from an alienating and objectifying focus on the sign as a referent to an object—slavery—rather than a subject—the questing consciousness of the former slave. Tuskegee realism, ever respectful of Washington's much-heralded "gospel of the toothbrush," sanitizes the mouth of the speaking subject until it attains that acme of "unselfishness" which is, in Washington's eyes, the hallmark of every successful man of action.

Neither the rise of pragmatism in the slave narrative nor the articulation of Tuskegee realism in *Up from Slavery* exerted a profound impact on the idealism of the protest fiction that dominated much late nineteenth- and early twentieth-century black belletristic prose in America. Protest romances from Frances Ellen Watkins Harper's *Iola Leroy* (1892) to Du Bois's *The Quest of the Silver Fleece* (1911) answer the call that Pauline Hopkins delivered in the preface to her novel *Contending Forces* (1900): "We must ourselves develop the men and women who will faithfully portray the inmost thoughts and feelings of the Negro with all the fire and romance which lie dormant in our history."[23] The problem with devoting the novel to romances of racial uplift, however, was that this could easily play into the hands of Tuskegee realism. Washington would have been happy to see the novel in its place, as a defensive, (merely) inspirational reaction to unjust realities.[24] The way to combat Tuskegee realism was not to justify romance, however well intentioned. Black wordsmiths needed to decertify—literally, to make *un*certain—the "real, solid foundation" on which Tuskegee realism claimed its hegemony. This is what happens in two prominent fictive texts of this period, Charles W. Chesnutt's *The Conjure Woman* (1899) and James Weldon Johnson's *The Autobiography of an Ex-Coloured Man* (1912).

As fictive autobiographies, both of these books exploit the anxiety that Washington expressed about biography as a representation of "a real man or a real thing." *The Conjure Woman* purports to be a collection of dictated slave narratives transcribed by a white entrepreneur from Ohio. However, by mediating his intention through Uncle Julius McAdoo's narratives and the conflicting interpretations of them offered by the Ohioan and his wife, Chesnutt made it hard for many readers to tell what the man behind all these masks really meant. Reviewers who did not know that Chesnutt was an Afro-American (neither Chesnutt nor his publishers mentioned this fact when *The Conjure Woman* came out) extrapolated from the text an implied author who, though a Northerner, had thoroughly immersed himself in the local color of the South and had written to entertain his white readership with the quaint customs and folklore of the southern Negro. Comparatively few reviewers perceived a "dark side" and tragic note in Chesnutt's representation of the slavery past.[25] The disparity between the two implied authors attributed to *The Conjure Woman* demonstrated that the real is not a constant but a function of words like "Negro" and "white" which are themselves but traces of racial *différance* in the cultural text of the racist American reading community.

Even more destabilizing of black biographical reality is Johnson's *Autobiography of an Ex-Coloured Man*. Published anonymously, the novel was designed by its author to be taken as a real, not a fictive, work. Most reviewers, as well as a large part of the black reading community,[26] were taken in by the *vraisemblance* of the novel, which, if one were to analyze it in detail, reads almost like a catalog of the stock in trade of nineteenth-century realism. What distinguishes the ex-colored man as a persona is not his storytelling but his leisurely digressions from the facts of his life into the realm of social and cultural commentary. His breadth of experience, his criticism of whites and blacks alike, and his almost Olympian detachment from racial loyalties give him an objectivity toward the whole race question that sounds almost Tuskegean. Moreover, Washington would surely have concurred with the ex-colored man's regretful judgment of his having passed for white as a selfish and socially unproductive act. An even more obvious invocation of the Tuskegee line comes at the end of the novel, when Washington himself makes a cameo appearance representing all the "earnestness and faith" of a progressive race, as contrasted with the self-protective cynicism of the ex-colored man.

What do these apparent endorsements of Tuskegee realism mean, however, if the narrator who makes them is not a "real man"? Does the fictiveness of the narrator invalidate the authority of what he says? Does fictive language have less—or perhaps more—performative potential than natural language?[27] Did Johnson invent a fictive character like the ex-colored man out of a belief that such a vehicle could actually represent certain facts more fully and freely than an actual man? If so, is this a testimonial to the strength of the Afro-American novel or the weakness of Afro-American autobiography? However we answer these questions posed by the problematic "author-function" of *The Autobiography of an Ex-Coloured Man*, we can see clearly enough that the novel does not leave unscathed many of the assumptions about realism—how to recognize it, how to read it—that Washington held dear.[28] If Johnson wrote the ex-colored man's story with no other purpose than to unveil the cultural conventions that predisposed his readership to believe an "autobiography" by a doubly phony white man over a novel authored by a real black man, namely, Johnson himself, his effort must be considered a signal success in the history of Afro-American autobiography, as well as fiction.

The pragmatic reassessment of slavery and the rise of Afro-American realism illustrate a process of revisionism at work in black narrative of the late nineteenth century that exempted virtually nothing in the past from being remade anew. Whatever black reality *was* historically, whatever one generation of black narrators said it was, their successors refused to be bound by it. First pragmatic slave narrators, then the Tuskegee realists, and then novelists like Chesnutt and Johnson insisted on their right to reappropriate the signifying potential of black reality and, through what we might call deconstructive acts, prepare the discursive ground once again for a new assay of the basis on which a usable truth could be constructed. From the perspective of the New Negroes of the Harlem Renaissance, Johnson had only begun to probe the deeper resources of subjective consciousness in *The Autobiography of an Ex-Coloured Man*; Chesnutt had only glimpsed the import of black folk culture in the magical realism of *The Conjure Woman*. Nevertheless, in their revisionistic attitude toward prevailing notions of the real, and in their emphasis on reality as a function of consciousness mediated through language, these were enabling texts. They not only pointed new directions for the Harlem Renaissance; they bore witness to the postbellum slave narrators' determination to keep the past alive and meaningful to the present. In short, the work of Chesnutt and Johnson helped preserve Afro-American realism as a literary tradition, a bridge between the antebellum and modern eras, that makes Tuskegee available for the Invisible Man to reinvent and enables the transposing of the "apparently incoherent" slave songs of Douglass's *Narrative* into the *Song of Solomon*.

NOTES

1. *Narrative of the Life of Frederick Douglass, an American Slave, Written by Himself*, edited and with an introduction by Houston A. Baker, Jr. (New York: Viking Penguin, 1982), 113.

2. *The Autobiographical Writings*, vol. 1 of *The Booker T. Washington Papers* ed. Louis R. Harlan and John W. Blassingame (Urbana: University of Illinois Press, 1972), 222–23. Subsequent quotations from *Up from Slavery* are from this edition, cited parenthetically in text and notes.

3. Orlando Patterson, *Slavery and Social Death* (Cambridge: Harvard University Press, 1982), 38–45.

4. For a brief, introductory look at the subject, see my "Forgotten Voices

of Afro-American Autobiography, 1865–1930," *A/B: Auto/Biography Studies* 2 (Fall 1986): 21–27.

5. Theodore Parker, "The American Scholar," in *The American Scholar*, ed. George Willis Cooke, vol. 8 of *Centenary Edition of Theodore Parker's Writings* (Boston: American Unitarian Association, 1907), 37.

6. For further discussion of the relationship of mid-nineteenth-century black American literature to romanticism, see William L. Andrews, "The 1850s: The First Afro-American Literary Renaissance," in William L. Andrews, *Literary Romanticism in America* (Baton Rouge: Louisiana State University Press, 1981), 38–60.

7. The overwhelming majority of slave narratives, both before and after the Civil War, were written or dictated by men. Of the approximately 115 slave narratives separately published in the United States and Great Britain between 1760 and 1930, only thirteen were dictated or written by black women. For this reason my examples of typical slave narrators are male.

8. *Narrative of the Life and Adventures of Henry Bibb* (New York: By the Author, 1849), 17.

9. James W. C. Pennington, *The Fugitive Blacksmith*, in *Great Slave Narratives*, ed. Arna Bontemps (Boston: Beacon Press, 1968), 237.

10. The slave's binary view of the world was not his or her creation alone, however. The "we-they" distinction that allowed whites to view and treat slaves as utterly other preceded and to a large extent compelled the diametrical image of the world in the slave's eyes. See Winthrop D. Jordan, *White over Black: American Attitudes toward the Negro, 1550–1812* (Baltimore: Penguin Books, 1969), 94–97.

11. See especially the chapter entitled "The Uses of Marginality, 1850–1865" in my *To Tell a Free Story: The First Century of Afro-American Autobiography, 1760–1865* (Urbana: University of Illinois Press, 1986), 167–204.

12. The means of emancipation among the postbellum narrators were many. A few postbellum slave narratives recount the rebellion and flight of fugitives well before the Civil War. See, for example, Mattie J. Jackson, *The Story of Mattie J. Jackson*, ed. L. S. Thompson (Lawrence, Mass.: L. S. Thompson, 1866) or *Autobiography of James L. Smith* (Norwich, Conn.: By the Author, 1881). A few other narrators preferred to purchase their freedom rather than run away. See Elizabeth Keckley, *Behind the Scenes: Thirty Years a*

Slave and Four Years in the White House (New York: G. W. Carleton, 1868) or Elisha Green, *Life of the Rev. Elisha W. Green* (Maysville, Ky.: Republican Printing, 1888). Some narrators recall having bided their time in slavery until the upheavals of war had so weakened their masters' control that slipping away to the Union army was relatively safe. See Allen Parker, *Recollections of Slavery Times* (Worcester, Mass.: Charles W. Burbank, 1895) or Louis Hughes, *Thirty Years a Slave* (Milwaukee: By the Author, 1896). Still others waited until formal emancipation came with the collapse of the Confederacy. See Jacob Stroyer, *My Life in the South* (Salem, Mass.: Newcomb & Gauss, 1898), Rev. I. E. Lowery, *Life on the Old Plantation in Ante-bellum Days* (Columbia, S.C.: State Company, 1911), or Monroe F. Jamison, *Autobiography and Work of Bishop M. F. Jamison, D.D.* (Nashville: By the Author, 1912).

13. Henry Clay Bruce, *The New Man: Twenty-nine Years a Slave, Twenty-nine Years a Free Man* (York, Pa.: P. Anstadt & Sons, 1895), 38–39.

14. George Henry, *Life of George Henry* (Providence, R.I.: By the Author, 1894), 23.

15. Orlando Patterson points out that because slavery was understood as a state of dishonor, the denial of power or value to a slave followed logically. When a slave narrator like Douglass speaks of rebellion restoring his sense of "manhood," he is actually alluding to his crucial desire for honor, on which every free man's sense of individual power and social value depends. See *Slavery and Social Death*, 10–13. In the postbellum slave narrative, the same acute sense of the importance of acquiring honor in an inherently dishonorable condition is prevalent, but the mode of achieving it is usually not Douglass's, often because of extenuating circumstances such as marriage or family ties.

16. See William Craft, *Running a Thousand Miles for Freedom*, in *Great Slave Narratives*, ed. Arna Bontemps (Boston: Beacon Press, 1969), 272.

17. William James, "What Pragmatism Means," in *American Thought: Civil War to World War I*, ed. Perry Miller (New York: Holt, Rinehart, and Winston, 1954), 169.

18. Much of the despair registered in the slave narratives of the late antebellum era stems from their writers' conviction that American history was not progressive because slavery held the process of American social and political evolution in thrall. In search of historical precedent for their message, most antebellum slave narrators buttressed their narratives in mythical history as

recorded in the Bible, which showed how God had delivered the people of Israel from their bondage. Only after emancipation did the slave narrative incorporate a historical consciousness that chronicles progressive change at work in contemporary America. In the late nineteenth century, as black sociopolitical prospects declined, the postbellum slave narrator often turned for consolation back to the slave past, partly to remind himself and his readers of how far the race had really come, and partly to recover something valuable and sustaining to his present struggles.

19. Washington's Atlanta Compromise address evokes the sentimental image of the slave "whose fidelity and love you have tested in days when to have proved treacherous meant the ruin of your firesides" not simply to pander to white stereotypes but to exploit them in an argument that pictures the freedmen and freedwomen as builders, not destroyers, of the South in the past and the future (p. 332). Washington was by no means unique among postbellum slave narrators in stressing the constructive role of slaves in building the Old South and making possible the aristocratic tradition of which the New South liked to boast. See, for instance, John Quincy Adams, *Narrative of the Life of John Quincy Adams, When in Slavery, and Now as a Freeman* (Harrisburg, Pa.: By the Author, 1872), 46–47.

20. See August Meier, *Negro Thought in America: 1880–1915* (Ann Arbor: University of Michigan Press, 1963), 85–99.

21. "I remember that the first colored man whom I saw who knew something about foreign languages impressed me at that time as being a man of all others to be envied" (p. 256).

22. White suspicion of the veracity of slave narrators is almost as old as the slave narrative itself, which is one reason why there are so many authenticating documents in *Up from Slavery*. See Robert B. Stepto, *From Behind the Veil* (Urbana: University of Illinois Press, 1979), 3–31.

23. Pauline Hopkins, *Contending Forces* (1900; reprint, Carbondale: Southern Illinois Press, 1978), 14.

24. Hazel Carby points out that when Washington saw a novelist like Hopkins as a threat, he took forceful action—by buying the organ, *The Colored American Magazine*, in which her novels were first serialized.

25. I base these generalizations on the critical response to *The Conjure Woman* which I found on my perusal of the scrapbooks of contemporary

press clippings and reviews of that book housed in the Chesnutt Collection of the Fisk University Library, Nashville, Tennessee.

26. In his autobiography, Johnson recalls a dinner party at which he met a man who obliquely confessed to having authored *The Autobiography of an Ex-Coloured Man*! See *Along This Way* (1933; reprint, New York: Viking, 1968), 238–39.

27. I use the terms "fictive" and "natural" as Barbara Herrnstein Smith uses them in *On the Margins of Discourse* (Chicago: University of Chicago Press, 1978), 15, 21–25.

28. I use the term "author-function" as Michel Foucault defines it in "What Is an Author?" in Josué V. Harari, ed., *Textual Strategies* (Ithaca: Cornell University Press, 1979), 141–60.

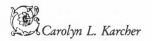Carolyn L. Karcher

Lydia Maria Child's
A Romance of the Republic

AN ABOLITIONIST VISION OF
AMERICA'S RACIAL DESTINY

The half century that began with the launching of a radical anti-slavery crusade in the 1830s and culminated in the abandonment of Reconstruction in the 1870s has justly been viewed as one of the most critical periods in American history. Both the major successes of the era—the abolition of slavery and the enfranchisement of the black man—and its failures—the substitution of peonage for slavery in the South; the persistence of virulent racial bigotry and discrimination, relegating blacks to the status of a permanent underclass throughout the nation; and the breakdown of an alliance that had sought to conjoin the liberation struggles of white women and people of color—have had momentous consequences, which still haunt us.

Antislavery fiction furnishes a particularly illuminating perspective on the constraints that prevented abolitionists from envisioning viable solutions to the problem they grappled with for five decades: how to create a truly egalitarian America. As a genre largely shaped by middle-class white women, it reflects the complex relationship between the patriarchal system that victimized women and the racial slave system that victimized blacks. At the same time, the conventions of antislavery fiction delimit the parameters within which women had to confine their exploration of slavery and their attempts to imagine alternative social orders. By dictating a romance plot involving refined heroines, by proscribing frank treatment of sexuality and violence, and by imposing a white middle-class code of values as the ideal toward which all were to aspire, antislavery fiction reproduces and may well have reinforced the ideological assumptions that marginalized the masses of American blacks and circumscribed the freedom of white women.

I would like to focus this discussion on Lydia Maria Child's 1867 novel, *A Romance of the Republic*, because it specifically offers a post–Civil War abolitionist vision of America's racial destiny. As Child confided to her friends, her intention was to address the issue of racial prejudice, which she had long recognized as crucial for the American people to tackle if they were to undo the evil of slavery and fulfill the egalitarian promise of their national creed. "Having fought against *slavery* till I saw it go down in the Red Sea," she wrote, "I wanted to do something to undermine *prejudice*; and there is such a universal passion for novels, that more can be done in that way, than by the ablest arguments, and the most serious exhortations."[1]

At the outset of her career as an abolitionist, Child had devoted the final chapter of her pioneering 1833 book, *An Appeal in Favor of That Class of Americans Called Africans*, to "Prejudices against People of Color, and Our Duties in Relation to This Subject." Heading the list of the discriminatory statutes and practices for which she had castigated her fellow northerners was an "unjust law" forbidding "marriages between persons of different color."[2] Thus it seems fitting that Child should have made interracial marriage her chief metaphor for the egalitarian partnership of America's diverse races to which she summoned her compatriots in *A Romance of the Republic*.

Actually, however, the possibility that intermarriage might provide a solution to America's race problem, by promoting assimilation and ultimately eliminating racial categories altogether, had occurred to Child even before her conversion to abolition. Indeed, the romance plot itself may have suggested the metaphor of interracial marriage to her, for she stumbled on it in her very first literary endeavor, an 1824 novel titled *Hobomok*, in which an Anglo-American woman elopes with an Indian. Although the heroine eventually leaves her Indian husband when her long-lost betrothed, an Englishman, reappears, the assimilation of her half-Indian son into Anglo-American society offers an alternative to race war and Indian genocide, which most other frontier romances of the 1820s and 1830s rationalize as inevitable.[3]

Of course interracial marriage represents a subversion, rather than a fulfillment, of the romance plot's traditional function—to reestablish the harmony of a social order threatened with disruption. While adhering to the convention of symbolically reconciling class antagonisms through marriage, the marriage in question violates one of the society's primary taboos. Nevertheless, to the extent that it ratifies the central institution of patriarchy and upholds the norms of the dominant race, interracial marriage does not fundamentally challenge a social order that subordinates women to men, people of color to whites, and the working classes to the bourgeoisie. Instead, it merely provides a means of gradually absorbing people of color into the white middle-class mainstream. This duality lies at the heart of Child's *A Romance of the Republic*, which encapsulates both the strengths and the limitations of abolitionism as an antiracist movement, and which poignantly reveals how effectively women's continuing subjection to patriarchal canons served to thwart the restructuring of American society along egalitarian lines.

The plot of the novel had been germinating in Child's mind ever since the appearance of Richard Hildreth's *The Slave; or, Memoirs of Archy Moore* (1836), generally credited with having inaugurated the American antislavery novel. "If I were a man," Child had avowed in a panegyric published in *The Liberator,* "I would rather be the author of that work, than of anything ever published in America" (March 18, 1837; *CC,* 5/118). Yet a woman writer, Child realized, could not adopt the viewpoint of a rebellious male fugitive and narrate his story in the first person—the device Hildreth had used so successfully. Besides, she noted, any work that "took the *same* ground as Archy Moore would seem utterly tame in comparison" (*CC,* 5/120). Not until 1841 did Child solve the problem of formulating a fictional strategy better suited to both a woman writer and the female audience she sought to move. That strategy, first embodied in a short story titled "The Quadroons,"[4] was to personify the evils of slavery in an archetype that has come to be known as the "tragic mulatto." Light-skinned and genteel, the archetypal "tragic mulatto" heroine either dies of grief when her white lover abandons her for a wife of his own race, or she becomes a "raving maniac" when sold to a profligate upon the death of her master—the fates, respectively, of Rosalie and her daughter Xarifa in "The Quadroons."[5]

Child herself found the story embarrassingly sentimental, as she admitted to her fellow abolitionist Maria Chapman. "You . . . will laugh at it heartily," she conceded ruefully, "but the young and romantic will like it. It sounds, in sooth, more like a girl of sixteen, than a woman of forty; and I can give no rational account how I happened to fall into such a strain. The fact is, I was plagued to death for a subject, and happened to hit upon one that involved much love-making" (CC, 12/292).

Did Child also sense that her plot, far from counteracting taboos against interracial marriage, subtly reinforced them? Such would seem to be her motive for turning a tragedy of miscegenation into a romance of interracial marriage twenty-five years later, when she finally fulfilled her ambition to write an antislavery novel.

In the intervening decades, Child digested the lessons of two black-authored narratives depicting sexual relations between white masters and quadroon slaves: William Wells Brown's *Clotel* (1853) and Harriet A. Jacobs's *Incidents in the Life of a Slave Girl* (1861), both of which acknowledged a debt to Child. Brown not only based a significant portion of *Clotel* on "The Quadroons," but lifted whole pages from the story.[6] Thus, his departures from Child's plot assume special significance. At two key points, where "The Quadroons" tends to exonerate the white lover Edward and his legal wife Charlotte and to assign the slave heroine Rosalie too passive a role, Brown discards his model. Instead of having Clotel die of grief when her lover Horatio marries, for example, Brown has Horatio's wife insist that he sell his former mistress to a slave trader. Subsequently, Brown allows Clotel to escape her new master and seek out her daughter, dying in the attempt to win freedom for them both. Brown also counterbalances Clotel's tragedy with the good fortune of her sister Althesa, redeemed from slavery by an honorable young physician from Vermont, who makes her his wife. Child would take the hint on recasting her plot in *A Romance of the Republic*, where her octoroon heroine, sold as well as abandoned by her lover, no longer dies of grief but escapes. Paralleling Clotel's effort to rescue her daughter, Child's Rosabella rescues her son by exchanging him in the cradle with the infant born to her lover's white bride. And like Brown's Althesa, Rosabella ends up marrying an up-right New Englander.[7]

The insights Child gained into the white slaveholder's psychology as a result of editing *Incidents in the Life of a Slave Girl* for Harriet A. Jacobs further strengthened the novel. Jacobs's frank account of her master's philandering, her mistress's jealousy, and her white lover's failure to keep his promises of freeing her children inform Child's characterizations of the slaveholder Gerald Fitzgerald and his wife Lily.

The crucial change Child made in her plot, of course, was to transform her light-skinned heroine from a tragic symbol of a proscribed race's sexual exploitation into a triumphant symbol of a nation's rebirth as a racially integrated society. Whether drawing her inspiration from Brown's Althesa, or, as she claimed, from real-life cases she had encountered of light-skinned fugitives who had married northern white men and were successfully passing as whites (*CC*, 67/1789), Child experimented with this redefinition of the "tragic mulatto" archetype in an 1858 story for the *Atlantic Monthly* titled "Loo Loo: A Few Scenes from a True History." There she introduced a preliminary version of the character who was to serve in *A Romance of the Republic* as her main vehicle for redeeming American society from the sin of slavery— the high-minded New Englander Alfred Noble, who ultimately marries the octoroon heroine he has saved from the claimants of her white father's property.

While preparing the way for a reappropriation of the mulatto figure to the end of advocating interracial marriage, however, "Loo Loo" reveals even more clearly than *A Romance of the Republic* how problematic a metaphor marriage would prove for the equal partnership of whites and blacks. Significantly, Noble steps into the place of Loo Loo's father, buying her when she is only nine years old and taking charge of her education. He then proceeds to reenact her father's sins. He, too, fails to manumit Loo Loo, despite the precariousness of her position in New Orleans, where he has settled. He even enters into concubinage with her, as her father had with her mother. Only after his bankruptcy in the panic of 1837 once again subjects Loo Loo to confiscation by creditors does Noble at last fulfill his intention of taking her north and marrying her. Under the circumstances, marriage hardly frees Loo Loo from patriarchal domination. Quite the contrary, Loo Loo embraces her dependent status all too readily. For the rest of her life, she continues to charm her husband by repeating the words that cemented their relationship at the outset: "I thank you, Sir, for buying me."[8]

A Romance of the Republic fuses the marriage plot of "Loo Loo" with the sexual exploitation narratives of "The Quadroons," *Clotel*, and *Incidents in the Life of a Slave Girl*. Like Child's *Appeal in Favor of That Class of Americans Called Africans*, this ambitious novel attempts both to present a wide-ranging, historically grounded critique of slavery and to suggest ways of overcoming the legacy of racism the institution has left.

The parentage of the novel's heroines recapitulates the history of American slavery. Rosabella and Flora Royal are the dazzlingly beautiful octoroon daughters of a Bostonian merchant, settled in New Orleans, and of a "half French, half Spanish" mother who, unbeknown to them, was born a slave in the French West Indies.[9] Just as the Spaniards introduced slavery into the West Indies and transplanted it to the mainland, with the French following in their wake, so the Spanish grandfather of Rosabella and Flora bought their mulatto grandmother in the French West Indies and took her to St. Augustine. Just as Anglo-Americans inherited slavery from the Spaniards, so Mr. Royal has in turn bought his slave mistress Eulalia from her Spanish father. Royal's New England background emphasizes yet another historical fact—the key role Yankee slave traders played in establishing the foundations of the South's plantation economy. His emigration to the South and subsequent entanglement in slavery, finally, illustrate the connection between slavery and patriarchy, between southern and northern systems of caste, class, and economic exploitation: originally engaged to the daughter of a Boston aristocrat, Royal went South to make his fortune when her father objected to her marrying a poor clerk without prospects and forced her into a match with a wealthy man she did not love.

Child must already have conceived her heroines by the time she prophesied in an 1865 letter to the *National Anti-Slavery Standard*: "Some future composer will give us the Prayer of a *black* Moses in tones as inspired as those of Rossini. Operas will embody the romantic adventures of beautiful fugitive slaves; and the prima donna will not need to represent an Octoroon, for men will come to admire the dark, glowing beauty of tropical flora, as much as the violets and lilies of the North" (*CC*, 61/1616). In all but one respect, *A Romance of the Republic* fulfills that prophecy. Based partially on Rossini's opera *Norma*, it features the "romantic adventures of beautiful fugitive slaves" and sets the "dark, glowing beauty" of the "tropical" heroines Flora and Rosabella against the pallid charms of a northern rival named Lily and the sober tints of a perpetually violet-clad northern matron named Lila. The prima donna it brings on stage for the role of Norma, however, remains an octoroon. Precisely because her aim was to undermine the color prejudice that kept American audiences from accepting a black prima donna, Child felt she had to persist in her practice of using one with no discernible African ancestry. Unfortunately, this concession to the bigotry she had explicitly criticized in her letter to the *Standard*, far from promoting the valorization of African beauty, has the effect of endorsing an ethnocentric preference for approximations of white beauty.

Child's dilemma arose partly from her commitment to a strategy of indirection. As she had long ago divulged to an abolitionist friend, her favorite approach was to "attack bigotry with 'a troop of horse shod with felt'; that is . . . to *enter* the wedge of general principles, letting inferences unfold themselves very gradually."[10] True, such a strategy did not of itself require a heroine who could pass for white. In his 1857 novel *The Confidence-Man*, for example, Herman Melville subverts the very concept of race through a character who masquerades interchangeably as a black and as a white and whose actual racial identity remains unfathomable.[11] Although *The Confidence-Man* was doubtless too obscure to have served Child as a model, she could have found other alternatives to the double-edged conventions of antislavery fiction had she sought them in the slave narratives with which she was so familiar. Why, then, did she refrain from following the lead of

Harriet Jacobs's *Incidents in the Life of a Slave Girl*? Parodying the conventions of the romance plot, Jacobs had explicitly signaled her departure from its traditional denouement: Reader, my story ends with freedom; not in the usual way, with marriage."[12] If the twist appeals to the modern reader who idealizes feminist independence, however, it does not lend itself to Child's purpose of dramatizing the ex-slave's integration into American society. After all, the prejudice and restricted opportunities Jacobs continued to face in the North certainly did not constitute a happy ending to her story. As for Jacobs herself, she epitomized the light-skinned genteel victim of slavery, not the "dark, glowing beauty" of her African sister.

Child's goal, moreover, was to woo her readers into embracing blacks as equal partners. For the specter of racial strife, she wished to substitute the vision of family harmony. Given these metaphors, and her predilection for indirect modes of counteracting her readers' prejudices, the choices of a romance plot and light-skinned heroines were inevitable.

In keeping with her strategy of "letting inferences unfold themselves very gradually," Child introduces Rosabella and Flora to the reader without revealing their ancestry. This is the very tactic to which the girls' father resorts when he invites his Bostonian visitor and namesake, Alfred Royal King, home for an exhibition of his daughters' talents. "I had a desire to know first how my daughters would impress you, if judged by their own merits," Mr. Royal later explains (p. 18). Child obviously wishes the reader to react as King does: "He could not make these peculiarities [Rosa's golden complexion and wavy black hair] seem less beautiful to his imagination, now that he knew them as signs of her connection with a proscribed race. . . . Octoroons! He repeated the word to himself, but it did not disenchant him. It was merely something foreign and new to his experience, like Spanish or Italian beauty. Yet he felt painfully the false position in which they were placed by the unreasoning prejudice of society" (p. 14).

The first chapter raises the questions: Can this "unreasoning prejudice" be overcome? If not, what are the consequences for women like Rosabella and Flora? For American society at large?

Having fallen in love with Rosa after an evening of listening to her sing, King would like to be able to marry her, but he knows his invalid mother shares society's prejudice. Every time he returns in imagination to "that enchanting room" in Royal's house, "where the whole of life seemed to be composed of beauty and gracefulness, music and flowers . . . the recollection of Boston relatives [rises] up like an iceberg between him and fairy-land" (pp. 14, 25). The imagery suggests the heavy price a society must pay in cultural impoverishment, even frigidity and sterility, when it erects barriers against other races. King suffers keenly from the sensual deprivations of his New England environment and yearns for the aesthetic pleasures that Rosabella and Flora incarnate. For the moment, however, he finds the "impediments" to marriage "insurmountable."

In the slave South, as Mr. Royal knows all too well, the impediments are more than insurmountable, and the consequences for all parties are more drastic. The laws of Louisiana do not recognize interracial marriages, and since Mr. Royal never manumitted the girls' mother, Rosabella and Flora, too, are legally slaves. Unless he can fulfill his intention of taking them to France, their fate will be the concubinage that was their mother's—or worse. Personifying the dangers that threaten them is the dashing Georgia slaveholder Gerald Fitzgerald, who has been assiduously courting Rosa, to her father's dismay. "If I were the Grand Bashaw, I would have them both in my harem," Fitzgerald confides to King, as they leave the Royal house together (p. 12). In short, the racial proscriptions that make the North an iceberg make the South a harem.[13] The rest of the novel shows how this affects the family lives of both races. It also examines the impact of prejudice on various classes and ethnic groups and tests the possibilities for change.

Fitzgerald's fantasy of playing Grand Bashaw and setting up a harem with the Royal sisters turns out to be prophetic. A year after the soiree at the Royal home with which the novel opens, Mr. Royal dies bankrupt, and his daughters discover that they are property, to be sold for the benefit of creditors. When Fitzgerald proposes to spirit them away, they agree on condition that he first marry Rosa (their sheltered life having left them ignorant of Southern laws on this point). Some weeks later, Fitzgerald installs the girls in a secluded cottage on his Georgia sea-island plantation, which proves to be a more sinister version of their New Orleans household; it is "evident at a glance," Child pointedly remarks, that "the master of the establishment" has done his "utmost to make the interior of the dwelling resemble their old home as much as possible" (pp. 75-76).

The parallels between the Fitzgerald and Royal households extend further than the girls realize. Both are founded on lies. Rosa's marriage is no more legitimate than her mother's was, and she and Flora are once again slaves, while believing themselves to be free. In order to "obtain a legal ownership of them," without which he can "feel no security" about retaining them, Fitzgerald has arranged with Royal's creditors to pay twenty-five hundred dollars for the pretended fugitives, on the chance that he can track them down (pp. 67, 74). Both households consequently require concealment and isolation from society. In New Orleans, Mr. Royal had withdrawn from circles into which he could not bring his wife and had carefully shielded his daughters from contact with all but a few trusted friends. In Georgia, Fitzgerald keeps the sisters' very existence literally veiled in secrecy. On the plea that neither their whereabouts nor his participation in their escape must come to light, he insists that Rosa and Flora remain "entirely out of sight of houses and people" and charges them to "wear thick veils" whenever they venture out, taking care "never to raise them" in front of strangers (pp. 79, 81).

Well might Fitzgerald boast that he does not "envy the Grand Bashaw his Circassian beauties" (p. 84), for he, too, enjoys the exclusive possession of women confined to his premises, shrouded in purdah, and reduced to the function of entertaining their master with song and dance. His emulation of a Turkish sultan whose prize harem slaves were Caucasians involves keen ironies. The reversal of cultural roles recalls that whites were once enslaved by the dark-skinned peoples they now despise, and the adoption by a Christian of Islamic practices makes a mockery out of the argument that slavery served to Christianize the African.[14] Only one of the Grand Bashaw's privileges continues to elude Fitzgerald—a plurality of wives. Before long, he takes the last steps toward translating his fantasy into reality, first by demanding sexual favors from Flora, ultimately by acquiring a legal bride.

Through the details identifying the Royal sisters as unwitting harem slaves, Child suggests still another parallel between the Royal and Fitzgerald households. In both, patriarchy and slavery are synonymous, the women being in every sense the "property" of the household's male head.

Child unmistakably equates the two institutions. "Patriarchism," she had pointed out in an article advocating woman suffrage, had originated as a system of "protection," giving the "husband and father" absolute power over "wives and children" in exchange for defending them against enemies (*CC*, 66/1759). It is thus no coincidence that Fitzgerald acquires his power over Rosa by offering to protect her from the creditors, auctioneers, and lascivious purchasers who menace her: "He smiled as he thought to himself that, by saving her from such degradation, he had acquired complete control of her destiny" (pp. 66–67). Come what may, he assures Rosa, "you shall never be the property of any man but myself" (p. 61). When she recoils with indignation from a word that smacks of the slavery she is trying to escape, Fitzgerald substitutes the more acceptable language of patriarchy: "I merely meant to express the joyful feeling that you would be surely mine, wholly mine." Because Rosa has been brought up to acquiesce in the patriarchal assumption that a wife belongs surely and wholly to her husband, she has not learned the lesson Child strives to impress on her reader—that the same reality underlies both forms of discourse.

In the Royal household patriarchy had worn a benign face, and the patriarch's true relationship to his womenfolk had lain hidden. In the Fitzgerald household, the meaning of patriarchy is spelled out. The patriarch discloses the face of the slavemaster, and the protective husband steps forward as the Grand Bashaw.

Reiterating the moral of Royal's story, Child shows that the same relationship between patriarchy and slavery obtains in the North. Like the fiancée Royal has had to renounce, Fitzgerald's bride Lily is the daughter of a wealthy Bostonian merchant, for whom her marriage represents a mere financial and social arrangement. As ignorant of her status as Rosa is of hers, and unaware of Rosa's existence, to boot, the new Mrs. Fitzgerald does not realize that she, too, is a victim of patriarchy and slavery—that her husband has bought her only for her father's money, and that her father, in turn, has sold her for her husband's plantation and his own business prospects in the South. In fact Lily shares the Boston aristocracy's virulent racism and proslavery sympathies. Yet she will learn that her fate is inextricably intertwined with Rosa's. Long after Rosa's escape from slavery and Fitzgerald's death at the hands of a slave whose wife he molested, Lily discovers that their son, born within a week of Rosa's, was exchanged in the cradle with him and is now a slave, whereas the son she has brought up as hers is a member of the race she has taught him to despise.

While the first phase of the novel explores the interconnections among slavery, racism, and patriarchy, and assesses the price American society must pay for its oppression of blacks, the second phase attempts to ascertain whether the American people can arrest the cycle of wrongs they have set in motion, transcend the prejudices that poison their society, and rebuild their Republic on a foundation of freedom and equality for all. Through a cast of characters representing a broad cross section of the American public, Child suggests different answers.

At one end of the spectrum are those who show no capacity for growth, even in the face of revelations that transform their social reality. The most tragic example is Lily Fitzgerald. Her impulse is simply to continue pretending that Gerald is her son. "I never will give him up," she insists. "He has slept in my arms. I have sung him to sleep. I taught him all his little hymns and songs. He loves me; and I will never consent to take a second place in his affections" (p. 362).

Her loyalty would be admirable, except that she refuses to draw any inferences from the disclosure of Gerald's racial identity. She also refuses to take any interest in the fate of her biological son. "It would be very disagreeable to me to have a son who had been brought up among slaves," she explains. "I have educated a son to my own liking, and everybody says he is an elegant young man. If you would cease from telling me that there is a stain in his blood, I should never be reminded of it" (p. 386). In short, for Lily Fitzgerald, appearances and forms are paramount. As long as Gerald looks and acts like a white gentleman, and passes for such in the eyes of the world, she can go on acknowledging him as her son. Should he ever publicly identify himself as black or take a "colored wife," however, she would sever their relationship, as she makes no bones about admitting (p. 420).

Lily's father, Mr. Bell, lacks even the limited ability to love that enables her to remain conditionally loyal to "her" son. On the contrary, he is quite prepared to disinherit Gerald on learning of his actual parentage. But when he finds out that his true grandson is a fugitive slave whom he has just had his agents track down and resell, Bell rages: "Do you suppose, sir, that a merchant of my standing is going to leave his property to negroes? . . . A pretty dilemma you have placed me in, sir. My property, it seems, must either go to Gerald, who you say has negro blood in his veins, or to this other fellow, who is a slave with a negro wife" (pp. 393–94).

The scene brilliantly sums up the mentality of the class Mr. Bell represents, and prophesies its doom. Integration and amalgamation, Child implies, are inevitable; regardless of their wishes, the Mr. Bells of America will not be able to keep their property to themselves, and the Republic's black children will inherit their rightful patrimony. At the same time, Child recognizes that no arguments or pleas will reconcile the Mr. Bells to destiny—that, heedless even of self-interest, they will destroy themselves rather than relent. Accordingly, Mr. Bell dies of an apoplectic fit.

At the opposite end of the spectrum Child places characters embodying a variety of solutions to the problem of undoing the legacy of slavery: young Gerald; Mr. Royal's former fiancée, Lila Delano; and the upright Bostonian, Alfred Royal King, who falls in love with Rosa in the first chapter.

The revelation of Gerald's origins and, soon thereafter, his encounter in the Union army with the white half brother who was sold into slavery in his place, gradually impel him to reexamine his assumptions about slavery, race, and inherited wealth. From his half brother, Gerald learns what it means to be a slave, laboring without reward for the benefit of idle masters. He also learns to reevaluate the relative worth of the slave and the "fine gentleman." He realizes, for example, that he, who has received so many advantages, has less to show for them and is less useful to society than his brother, who has taught himself to read and whose mechanical ingenuity puts him perpetually "in demand to make or mend something" (p. 408).

At the same time, Child uses the ironic reversals in the two brothers' situations to undermine racist theories about innate traits fitting blacks for slavery and whites for mastery. Here it is the "black" brother who is the gentleman and the white who is the slave. In features and coloring, moreover, the two are indistinguishable—all that differentiates them is the manners and skills each has acquired as a result of his circumstances. The point, of course, is that both men are products of their environment, rather than of their racial makeup, which, indeed, is so similar as to reduce racial categories to absurdity.[15]

Through Gerald, Child offers the hope that a portion, at least, of the northern and southern aristocracies founded on slavery can be taught to repudiate hierarchies of race and class ill-befitting a republic. Gerald himself does not participate in the reconstruction of American society after the Civil War, however. Perhaps embodying the destruction of slavery itself, he is killed in combat.

Of the characters who set new directions for the nation, the most interesting is Lila Delano. Widowed after an unhappy marriage with the man for whom her father forced her to break her engagement with Royal, Lila ends up playing the role of fairy godmother to Royal's daughter Flora, whom she helps escape from Fitzgerald's Georgia plantation and eventually adopts. Until her chance meeting with Flora on a visit to the South, Mrs. Delano has shared her class's racism and opposition to "anti-slavery agitation" (p. 155). Had Flora been recognizably black, she could never have won Mrs. Delano's sympathies, but her spontaneity, exuberance, and "impulsive naturalness" charm the older woman, who has recently lost a daughter, and the attachment proves strong enough to withstand the revelation that Flora is "allied to the colored race, and herself a slave" (pp. 146, 155). In the process of befriending Flora, Mrs. Delano comes to abjure her former prejudices and ultimately joins forces with the abolitionists.

The cultural transformation she undergoes is even more significant, heralding as it does the kinds of changes that Child hoped would result from an intermingling of races, classes, and cultures. At first Mrs. Delano tries to "educate [Flora] after the New England pattern" (p. 209). When Flora objects to her "nice ideas of conventional propriety," Mrs. Delano gradually begins to realize that her protégée, "with her strange history and unworldly ways, is educating me more than I can educate her" (pp. 151, 269). By the end of the novel she has not only overcome her social snobbishness; she has even refurbished her home according to Flora's "tropical" tastes (p. 287). In sum, through Mrs. Delano, Child suggests that the eradication of racial prejudice and the integration of blacks into American society will benefit whites at least as much as blacks, infusing warmth, color, and spontaneity into a culture suffering from overrefinement.[16]

Unfortunately, as a metaphor for the integration process, the adoption plot involving Mrs. Delano and Flora suffers from serious defects. First, though modeled on an actual episode in Child's life— her attempt to adopt a friendless young Spanish woman she had encountered in New York—it inescapably reproduces the built-in inequality of the parent-child relationship by defining the white godmother as the adult and her black protégée as the child.[17] Second, the cultural contrasts Child draws between Mrs. Delano and Flora tend to reinforce ethnic stereotypes. Mercurial and artistic, Flora thrills to opera, ballet, and painting, but she cannot be prevailed upon to tackle the heavy intellectual fare deemed essential to a New England education. "One might as well try to plough with a butterfly, as to teach her ancient history," concludes Mrs. Delano in frustration (p. 209). Third, the ideal of assimilation Child suggests effectually erases the ethnic identity of American blacks. They are to dissolve into American society, transforming the traditional melting pot into a spicier "*olla podrida*," or Spanish stew, but ceasing to exist as a distinct people.[18]

The same defects also mar Child's most radical solution to the problem of eliminating racial hierarchies and class divisions—the solution embodied by the Bostonian Alfred Royal King, who marries Rosa and enacts a small-scale version of the abolitionist program for Reconstruction. More than any other character, King epitomizes the fatal flaws in the abolitionist imagination, which the romance plot brings to the fore.

Initially, the marriage of King and Rosa seems to usher in a new social order, free not only of racial proscriptions, but of patriarchal restrictions on women's freedom. After all, to marry Rosa, King must surmount more than the Boston aristocracy's racial prejudice and social exclusiveness; he must also surmount patriarchal attitudes toward "tainted" women. Between the time he first meets and falls in love with Rosa and the time he finally proposes to her, she has been "the victim of a sham marriage" and, after her escape, has taken to the stage as an opera singer—a career regarded as little more respectable than prostitution (pp. 245–46). In repudiating "the merely external distinctions of this deceptive world," King repudiates external measures of sexual purity along with external badges of racial and social status. He even rises above asking his wife to sacrifice her career and the independence it gives her, though he does express the hope that she will take up concert singing in lieu of opera (p. 252).

Inexplicably, having provided this glimpse of an alternative to patriarchal marriage, Child turns her back on it. Rosa chooses rather to fill the traditional role of an upper-class wife, and from this point on, King comes to dominate the novel, while Rosa degenerates into helpless dependency. Their marriage becomes a paradigm of gender and race relations in the post–Civil War world, as King unilaterally takes the responsibility for undoing the evils slavery has entailed on the Royal, King, and Fitzgerald families.

Personifying the chief wrong King sets about righting is the half brother who has been enslaved in the place of Rosa's son Gerald. Although white, he faces the same problems as other ex-slaves do after emancipation, especially since his marriage to a mulatto makes it impossible for him to "pass."

Child realized that as long as the ex-slaves remained ignorant and trapped in menial positions, barriers of caste and class would continue to divide them from whites and prevent their integration into American society. Thus she considered it essential for the government to develop a concerted program for educating the freed slaves and providing them with remunerative employment and opportunities for advancement. This is exactly what King proceeds to do for Gerald's half brother, George Falkner, and his wife. He engages George as an agent in the Marseilles branch of his business, with the aim of later taking the young man into partnership. Meanwhile, Rosa has been teaching Mrs. Falkner to read, write, embroider, and play the piano, so that she will be "educated in a degree somewhat suitable to her husband's prospects" (p. 414). Ultimately, King intends to make full reparation to George for his enslavement by bequeathing to him a sum equal to his rightful share of the Bell-Fitzgerald inheritance, plus interest. The intended bequest is to be kept a secret, to avoid turning the Falkners' heads until their characters have been "formed by habits of exertion and self-reliance," but King stipulates that "this judicious process must not, of course, deprive the young man of a single cent that is due to him" (pp. 415–16).

In many respects King's plan to help blacks enter into their inheritance as American citizens goes further than the Reconstruction program eventually adopted by the government. It includes just compensation to blacks for their centuries of unrequited toil, and it promises black men full partnership in the business of running the country.

Yet it displays the same ideological limitations that doomed abolitionism, once the initial goal of ending slavery had been achieved. Its most glaring defect is paternalism—never, for example, does it occur to King to consult the Falkners before deciding what is best for them;

nor does he credit them with having already formed strong characters and "habits of exertion and self-reliance." Intertwined with that paternalism, once again, is the patriarchal concept of woman's role implicit in the education Mrs. Falkner receives—one "suitable to her husband's prospects." But above all, King's plan is predicated on the assumption, anachronistic as early as the 1850s, that American society provided "an almost perfect opportunity for social mobility."[19] As King himself put it in his parting advice to George Falkner: "If you are industrious, temperate, and economical, there is no reason why you should not become a rich man in time" (p. 436).[20] In short, King personifies the tragic contradiction between the abolitionist ideal of a classless society in which whites and blacks, men and women, enjoyed equal opportunities, and the racial, sexual, and class paternalism that continued to dominate their thinking and mar their prescriptions for reform.

Summing up the strengths and weaknesses of the vision *A Romance of the Republic* offers of America's destiny is the series of *tableaux vivants* in which the novel culminates, as the Royal sisters' reunited families celebrate the end of the Civil War. The progeny of the two families, as Flora remarks proudly to her husband Franz, a German immigrant who once clerked for Mr. Royal, are "a good-looking set . . . though they *are* oddly mixed up" (p. 432). They no longer fit any recognizable racial category, but show traces of "African and French, Spanish, American, and German" ancestry. The tableaux they stage clearly prefigure the future Child dreams of for her country.

The first represents the Republic that has risen out of the ashes of slavery. Incarnating that Republic and the racial amalgamation in which its destiny lies is the Kings' daughter Eulalia, clad in "ribbons of red, white, and blue, with a circle of stars round her head" (p. 440). In one hand she carries "the shield of the Union"; in the other, "the scales of Justice . . . evenly poised." By her side stands Flora's daughter Rosen Blumen, flourishing a "liberty-cap" and resting her hand "protectingly" on the head of the black child the family has most recently rescued from slavery. Complete with this kneeling figure, "looking upward in thanksgiving," the tableau recalls innumerable prints and statues commemorating the emancipation. Here the emancipators are themselves children of emancipated slaves, yet the class relations between the two groups persist. And once again, a hierarchy of color has reasserted itself.

The second tableau, in which a minor character, a white working-man who has served in the war, leads a company of black soldiers, emblematizes the solidarity of white workers and black slaves and pays tribute to the nation's first black regiments. The reality this tableau reflects is historically accurate, in that the commanders of those regiments were all white. There is no indication, however, that the future holds a more egalitarian alliance between white and black workers.

The last tableau, in which the freed slaves sing Whittier's "Boat Song," symbolizes the fusion of black and white cultures that an amalgamated Republic will bring about. An emancipation poem modeled on slave songs, the "Boat Song" reflects the growing interest abolitionists were taking in the rich oral culture blacks had forged out of their oppression. Indeed, the very year *A Romance of the Republic* was published, the first two major collections of slave songs appeared, both issued by abolitionists.[21] No doubt Child did not have access to these collections while writing her novel, but she had certainly read the songs included in the slave narratives of Frederick Douglass and William Wells Brown and in the *Atlantic Monthly* articles of Charlotte Forten.[22] That she chose to have the slaves sing not a song of their own composing but the pale imitation a white poet had produced of one, testifies starkly to the stranglehold that the genteel canons of white middle-class culture continued to exert on her imagination.

Ultimately, they prevented Child from imagining adequate alternatives to the social order she had so brilliantly anatomized. Though able to perceive the interconnections between slavery and patriarchy, racial and sexual proscriptions; though able to diagnose the cultural impoverishment resulting from racial exclusiveness, Child proved unable to extricate herself from conceptions rooted in the very systems she sought to discredit. As a metaphor for equal partnership, interracial marriage foundered on the manifest inequality of a patriarchal institution in which, as Child knew from painful experience, the nineteenth-century wife lost her individual identity under the law and became literally her husband's appendage.[23] Within literary conventions that veiled the realities of race, class, and gender relations and that necessitated euphemism and obliquity, Child found it impossible to envision a truly egalitarian, multicultural society.

NOTES

1. *The Collected Correspondence of Lydia Maria Child, 1817–1880*, ed. Patricia G. Holland, Milton Meltzer, and Francine Krasno (Millwood, N.Y.: Kraus Microform, 1980), 67/1789, 1797; 69/1847. Subsequent references will be given parenthetically in the text and notes, keyed to the abbreviation *CC*. References include both microfiche card number and letter number.

2. Lydia Maria Child, *An Appeal in Favor of That Class of Americans Called Africans (Boston: Allen and Ticknor,* 1833), 209.

3. Lydia Maria Child, *Hobomok, a Tale of Early Times* (Boston: Cummings, Hilliard, 1824). For a fuller analysis of *Hobomok* and the significance of its intermarriage plot, see my introduction to *"Hobomok" and Other Writings on Indians*, ed. Carolyn L. Karcher (New Brunswick: Rutgers University Press, 1986).

4. "The Quadroons" was first published in the 1842 volume of the antislavery gift book, *The Liberty Bell*. It has recently been reprinted in *The Other Woman: Stories of Two Women and a Man*, ed. Susan Koppelman (New York: Feminist Press, 1984), 1–12. Child's letter of December 1, 1841, to *The Liberty Bell*'s editor, Maria Chapman, indicates that she had finished the story by late 1841 (*CC*, 12/292).

5. I have discussed the limitations of the "tragic mulatto" archetype as a vehicle for antislavery protest in "Rape, Murder, and Revenge in 'Slavery's Pleasant Homes': Lydia Maria Child's Antislavery Fiction and the Limits of Genre," *Women's Studies International Forum* 9, no. 4 (1986): 330–31. See also Sterling A. Brown, *The Negro in American Fiction* (1937; reprint, Port Washington, N.Y.: Kennikat, 1968), 45–46; Barbara Christian, *Black Women Novelists: The Development of a Tradition, 1892–1976* (Westport, Conn.: Greenwood

Press, 1980), 22–23; and Alice Walker, *In Search of Our Mothers' Gardens: Womanist Prose* (New York: Harcourt Brace Jovanovich, 1983), 290–312.

6. Compare chapters 4 and 8 of William Wells Brown's *Clotel; or, The President's Daughter* (1853; reprint, New York: Macmillian, 1970) with "The Quadroons." These verbatim borrowings are also noted by William Edward Farrison, *William Wells Brown, Author and Reformer* (Chicago: University of Chicago Press, 1969), 224, 228, 325. Brown's plagiarism actually betrays his discomfort with the "tragic mulatto" theme. In the following passage, for example, it becomes apparent that he borrows Child's description of the refined mulatto heroine precisely because it conveys a white view of his own people that he does not share and therefore cannot articulate for himself: "The iris of her large dark eye had the melting mezzotinto, which remains the last vestige of African ancestry, and gives that plaintive expression, so often observed, and so appropriate to that docile and injured race" (p. 58). Significantly, Brown eliminated these plagiarized passages from his three later versions of the novel. On the changes Brown made in Child's plot, see Jean Fagan Yellin, *The Intricate Knot: Black Figures in American Literature, 1776–1863* (New York: New York University Press, 1972), 172.

7. Although Child's voluminous correspondence furnishes no direct evidence that she ever read *Clotel*, it is hard to believe that she could have overlooked the first novel published by an American black. Reviewed in *The Liberator* and the *National Anti-Slavery Standard*, the novel was reprinted in four different versions under different titles. In 1864, while working out the plot of *A Romance of the Republic*, Child would have had her attention drawn to the third version, *Clotelle: A Tale of the Southern States*, when it was advertised in the *National Anti-Slavery Standard* on February 20 and in several numbers of *The Liberator* beginning March 18. See Farrison, *William Wells Brown*, 229, 387. Appropriately, the last version, *Clotelle; or, the Colored Heroine*, appeared the same year as *A Romance of the Republic*.

8. Lydia Maria Child, "Loo Loo. A Few Scenes from a True History," *Atlantic Monthly* 1, 2 (May, June 1858): 801–12, 32–42. The quotation occurs in 1:802, 1:811, and 2:42.

9. Lydia Maria Child, *A Romance of the Republic* (Boston: Ticknor and Fields, 1867), 13, 19. Subsequent page references will be given parenthetically in the text.

10. *Lydia Maria Child: Selected Letters, 1817–1880*, ed. Milton Meltzer, Patricia G. Holland, and Francine Krasno (Amherst: University of Massachusetts Press, 1982), 109.

11. See my chapter on *The Confidence-Man* in *Shadow over the Promised Land: Slavery, Race and Violence in Melville's America* (Baton Rouge: Louisiana State University Press, 1980), 186–257.

12. Harriet A. Jacobs, *Incidents in the Life of a Slave Girl. Written By Herself*, ed. L. Maria Child (1861; reprint, ed. Jean Fagan Yellin, Cambridge, Mass.: Harvard University Press, 1987), 201.

13. Child also uses the trope of the Southern Plantation as harem in "Slavery's Pleasant Homes. A Faithful Sketch," *The Liberty Bell*, 4, (1843): 147–60.

14. Child discusses both the Circassians and the practices of the Turkish sultans in her two-volume work, *The History of the Condition of Women, in Various Ages and Nations* (Boston: John Allen, 1835), 1:43–47.

15. Child's use of this device should be compared with Twain's in *Pudd'nhead Wilson* (1894). She is careful to avoid the "blood will tell" interpretation of the two men's characters, not only by stressing the influence of environment more heavily than Twain does, but by portraying Gerald as an essentially good-hearted young man capable of outgrowing the defects of his slaveholder's upbringing. In contrast, Twain's Tom is an irredeemable villain. The device nevertheless remains double-edged, since the mechanical ingenuity, intelligence, and drive exhibited by Gerald's half brother could still be attributed by racist readers to his white identity.

16. The cultural contrasts Child draws between Mrs. Delano and Flora invite comparison with those Stowe draws between Miss Ophelia and Topsy. Like Child, Stowe views the New England character with a critical eye, accentuating its coldness and rigidity. Though sharing Child's attraction to the sensuousness, artistry, and color so many New Englanders saw in African, southern, and Mediterranean cultures, Stowe resolves the dialectic in New England's favor, at least where blacks are concerned. By dint of patience and hard work, Miss Ophelia ultimately succeeds in turning Topsy into a model New Englander. Topsy exerts no corresponding influence on Miss Ophelia. See Harriet Beecher Stowe, *Uncle Tom's Cabin; or, Life Among the Lowly* (1852; reprint, New York: NAL, 1966), chaps. 15, 20, 27, 43.

17. I am indebted to Jean Fagan Yellin for pointing this out in her commentary on a preliminary version of the present essay. My book in progress, *Lydia Maria Child: The Woman of Letters as Political Activist*, to be published by Oxford University Press, contains a more detailed discussion of Child's relationship with her Spanish protégée Dolores, among other autobiographical elements in *A Romance of the Republic*.

18. I am indebted for this insight to H. Bruce Franklin's critique of an early draft of the present article. *"Olla podrida"* is the phrase Child uses to describe the mixture of English, Spanish, and French that Flora and Rosa speak between themselves (pp. 32, 149). It refers to a Spanish stew combining many kinds of meat and vegetables, including spicy Spanish sausages.

19. Eric Foner, *Free Soil, Free Labor, Free Men: The Ideology of the Republican Party before the Civil War* (New York: Oxford University Press, 1970), 25.

20. Child preached the same message throughout her children's magazine, *The Juvenile Miscellany* (1826-34). See, for example, her biographical sketch "Benjamin Franklin" in the *Juvenile Miscellany* 2 (March 1827): 18-23.

21. Thomas Wentworth Higginson, "Negro Spirituals," *Atlantic Monthly* 19 (June 1867): 684-94; William Francis Allen, Charles Pickard Ware, and Lucy McKim Garrison, *Slave Songs of the United States* (New York: A. Simpson, 1867). For a superb discussion of those songs and their reception by nineteenth-century white audiences, see H. Bruce Franklin, *The Victim as Criminal and Artist: Literature from the American Prison* (New York: Oxford University Press, 1978), 73-98.

22. See *The Narrative of The Life of Frederick Douglass, An American Slave. Written by Himself* (1845; reprint, New York: Doubleday, 1963), chap. 2; Frederick Douglass, *My Bondage and My Freedom* (1855; reprint, New York: Dover, 1969), 252-53, 278-79; *Narrative of William W. Brown, a Fugitive Slave. Written by Himself* (Boston: Anti-Slavery Office, 1847), 51-52; and Charlotte Forten, "Life on the Sea Islands," *Atlantic Monthly* 13 (May/June 1864): 67-86.

23. According to nineteenth-century law, the married woman became "dead in the law" and was referred to as "femme couverte." Child raged against such legal consequences as the necessity for her husband to sign her will in order to make it a legal document. See Meltzer, Holland, and Krasno, *Lydia Maria Child: Selected Letters*, 279.

![ornamental decoration] *Arnold Rampersad*

Slavery and the Literary Imagination

DU BOIS'S *THE SOULS OF BLACK FOLK*

W. E. B. Du Bois's *The Souls of Black Folk* was a controversial book when it appeared in 1903, but few readers opposed to it could deny its originality and beauty as a portrait of the Afro-American people. In the succeeding years, the collection of essays lost little of its power, so that it remains acknowledged today as a masterpiece of black American writing. In 1918, the literary historian Benjamin Brawley still could feel in Du Bois's book "the passion of a mighty heart" when he hailed it as the most important work "in classic English" published to that time by a black writer.[1] About thirty years after its appearance, the poet, novelist, and NAACP leader James Weldon Johnson judged that Du Bois's work had produced "a greater effect upon and within the Negro race in American than any other single book published in this country since *Uncle Tom's Cabin.*"[2] With admiration bordering on reverence for the book, Langston Hughes recalled that "my earliest memories of written words are those of Du Bois and the Bible."[3] In the 1960s, the astute literary critic J. Saunders Redding weighed the impact of *Souls of Black Folk* on a variety of black intellectuals and leaders and pronounced it "more history-making than historical."[4] In 1973, Herbert Aptheker, the leading Du Bois editor and scholar, hailed the text as "one of the classics in the English language."[5]

These are fervent claims for a book of thirteen essays and a short story written by an academic who had been rigidly trained in history and sociology (especially at Harvard and the University of Berlin, where Du Bois did extensive doctoral work), and whose previous books had been an austere dissertation in history, *The Suppression of the African Slave-Trade to the United States*, and an empirical sociological study of urban blacks, *The Philadelphia Negro*. Clearly, however, *The Souls of Black Folk* was something other than academic history and sociology. If white academics and intellectuals mainly ignored its existence (although Henry James called it "the only Southern book of distinction published in many a year"), its impression was marked on the class of black Americans who provided the leadership of their race.[6] Among black intellectuals, above all, *The Souls of Black Folk* became a kind of sacred book, the central text for the interpretation of the Afro-American experience and the most trustworthy guide into the grim future that seemed to loom before their race in America.

The main cause of the controversy surrounding *The Souls of Black Folk* was its devastating attack on Booker T. Washington. The head of the Tuskegee Institute in Alabama was already a famous man when his autobiography *Up from Slavery* was published in 1901. His epochal compromise speech at the Atlanta Exposition in 1895 had catapulted him to the position of leading spokesman for his race before the white world, a friend of rich industrialists like Andrew Carnegie and a dinner guest in the White House of Theodore Roosevelt. Nevertheless, *Up from Slavery* reinforced Washington's authority to a significant extent. Above all, he has used the skeleton of the slave narrative form (that is, the story of a life that progresses from a state of legal bondage to a state of freedom and a substantial degree of self-realization) not only to describe his rise in the world but also to dramatize the heart of the Tuskegee argument that the salvation of Afro-America lay in self-reliance, conciliation of the reactionary white South, a surrender of the right to vote and the right to social equality, dependence on thrift and industriousness, and an emphasis on vocational training rather than the liberal arts in the education of the young. To these ideas, Du Bois and *The Souls of Black Folk* were unalterably opposed.

I wish to suggest here that perhaps the most important element in the making of Du Bois's book, which drew on his previously published material but also on fresh work, derived in significant degree from his full awareness of *Up from Slavery*. While this could hardly be an altogether novel suggestion—given Du Bois's attack on Washington in his book—the crucial area of difference between them has not been adequately recognized. I would argue that this crucial element involved Du Bois's acute sensitivity to slavery both as an institution in American history and as an idea, along with his distaste for Washington's treatment of the subject in *Up from Slavery*. To some extent Du Bois's book functions, in spite of its only partial status as an autobiography, as a direct, parodic challenge to certain forms and assumptions of the slave narrative (in all their variety) which had so aided Booker T. Washington's arguments. While it does so mainly to refute the major ideas in Washington's influential text, at the same time its contrariness of form is made obligatory by Du Bois's peculiar attitudes toward slavery.

The resulting book can be seen as marking Du Bois's sense (and that of the many writers and intellectuals influenced by him) of the obsolescence of the slave narrative as a paradigm for Afro-American experience, as well as the beginning of a reflexive paradigm, allied to the slave narrative, that leads the reader—and the race described in the book—into the modern Afro-American world. William L. Andrews has pointed out elsewhere in this book, in his essay on slavery and the rise of Afro-American literary realism, that postbellum slave narratives de-emphasized the hellishly destructive nature of slavery and offered it instead as a crucible in which future black manhood was formed. Du Bois's approach, I would argue, is in part a revival of the earlier, antebellum spirit of black autobiography and the slave narrative, but in more significant part also differs from that earlier spirit. In both the earlier and the later slave narratives there is progress for the black as he or she moves away from slavery. Du Bois's central point, as we shall see, is different.

For Booker T. Washington in *Up from Slavery*, slavery was not an institution to be defended overtly. Nevertheless, its evils had been much overstated, as he saw them, and its blessings were real. The evils, insofar as they existed, were to be acknowledged briefly and then forgotten. While this approach in some senses is to be expected of an autobiography by a man born only seven years before emancipation, it also underscores Washington's public attitude to American slavery in particular and to history in general. In Washington's considered view, neither slavery nor history is of great consequence—or, at the very least, of daunting consequence to any black man of sound character who properly trains himself for the demands of the modern world. In *Up from Slavery*, Washington writes flatly of "the cruelty and moral wrong of slavery," and he remarks conclusively about the former slaves that "I have never seen one who did not want to be free, or one who would return to slavery."[7] "I condemn it as an institution," he adds (*US*, 37). Tellingly, however, this condemnation springs from a need to clarify the major message about slavery in his chapter on his slave years, "A Slave among Slaves." The need itself springs from the patent ambiguity of Washington's view of slavery.

Whatever he intends to do, Washington stresses the fundamentally innocuous, almost innocent, nature of the institution. Of his white father (said to be a prosperous neighbor, who refused to acknowledge him) and of his poor, black mother (who sometimes stole chickens in order to feed herself and her children), Washington's judgment is the same. In lacking the courage or generosity to acknowledge his son, his father "was simply another unfortunate victim of the institution which the Nation unhappily had engrafted upon it at the time" (*US*, 30). In her thievery, his mother "was simply a victim of the system of slavery" (*US*, 31). Moreover, Washington's lack of hostility to his father allegedly reflected the complacent attitudes of other blacks to whites. There was no "bitter feeling toward the white people on the part of my race" about the fact that many whites were fighting as soldiers in the Confederate army to preserve slavery; where slaves had been treated "with anything like decency," they showed love and tenderness to their masters, even those in the military (*US*, 35). The chapter "A Slave among Slaves" ends with a striking tableau of the day of emancipation. Whites are sad not because of the loss of valuable property but "because of parting with those whom they had reared and who were in many ways very close to them" (*US*, 39). Blacks are initially ecstatic, but the older freedmen, "stealthily at first," return later to the "big house" to consult their former masters about their future (*US*, 40).

Doubtless sincere in his expressions of antipathy to slavery, Washington nevertheless emphasizes the benefits gained by blacks through the institution. "Notwithstanding the cruel wrongs inflicted upon us," he asserts, "the black man got nearly as much out of slavery as the white man did" (*US*, 37). With Afro-Americans comprising the most advanced community of blacks in the world (as Washington claimed), slavery was indisputably a fortunate act. Indeed, it was further proof of the notion that "Providence so often uses men and institutions to accomplish a purpose" (*US*, 37). Through all difficulties, Washington continues to derive faith in the future of black Americans by dwelling on "the wilderness through which and out of which, a good Providence has already led us" (*US*, 37).

For Washington, the acknowledgment of Providence piously marks his negation of the consequences of forces such as those of history, psychology, economics, and philosophy at play in the field of slavery. (Providence does not perform a more positive function in his scheme, in which there is little room for religious enthusiasm or spiritual complexity. Of religion and spirituality in *Up from Slavery* he writes: "While a great deal of stress is laid upon the industrial side of the work at Tuskegee, we do not neglect or overlook in any degree the religious and spiritual side. The school is strictly undenominational, but it is thoroughly Christian, and the spiritual training of the students is not neglected" [*US*, 135].) Willing to share in the belief that economic competition and greed had been at the root of slavery, and that slavery itself was ultimately the cause of the Civil War, he pushes no further into causes and effects even as he everywhere, as a champion of pragmatism, lauds the value of "facts" and the "need to look facts in the face" (*US*, 37). In his scheme, the mental legacy of slavery to the black freedman is not conflict, but a blank, a kind of tabula rasa on which is to be inscribed those values and skills that would serve the freedman best in the new age. Although he offers a critical view of the past of his people, "who had spent generations in slavery, and before that generations in the darkest heathenism," Washington in fact invites a vision of the Afro-American as black Adam (*US*, 71). This Adam is, in a way, both prelapsarian and postlapsarian. He is an Adam in the Eden of the South, with the world before him. He is also Adam who has fallen. The fall was slavery itself. Slavery, as seen in this context, is a "fortunate fall"—the fall by which Africans gained the skills and the knowledge needed for the modern world. But who is responsible for the fall? Who has sinned? The answer surely must be the black slave himself, since *Up from Slavery* places no blame on the white world. The failure to investigate the origins, the nature, and the consequences of slavery has led Washington to a subtle and yet far-reaching defamation of the African and Afro-American peoples.

The black American Adam, in his prelapsarian guise, and in the simplicity of his capabilities, must be protected from the fruit that would destroy him—in this case, knowledge in the form of classical learning. Otherwise, the black man may become a kind of Satan, excessively proud. Washington denounces the idea, apparently embraced eagerly by many blacks in the aftermath of the Civil War, "that a knowledge, however little, of the Greek and Latin languages would make one a very superior human being, something bordering almost on the supernatural" (*US*, 71–72). Inveighing against false black pride, he dismisses passionate black claims to the right to vote. The secret of progress appears to be regression. Deploring the mass black migration to the cities, he often wishes "that by some power of magic I might remove the great bulk of these people into the country districts and plant them upon the soil, upon the solid and never deceptive foundation of Mother Nature, where all nations and races that have ever succeeded have gotten their start" (*US*, 77). His garden is a priceless source of resuscitation. There, "I feel that I am coming into contact with something that is giving me strength for the many duties and hard places that await me out in the big world. I pity the man or woman who has never learned to enjoy nature and to get strength and inspiration out of it." (*US*, 173).

This refusal to confront slavery (or even the understandable association in the minds of many blacks of agricultural work with the terms of slavery) and this black variation on the myth of an American Adam make *Up from Slavery* an odd slave narrative according to either the antebellum or the postbellum model. Nevertheless, the hero moves from slavery to freedom and into his future as from darkness to light. Holding the story together is the distinction Washington quietly makes between himself and the other ex-slaves in general. He is the hero of a slave narrative. He sheds the dead skin of slavery, seeks an education, builds on it, and emerges as a powerful, fully realized human being, confident, almost invincible (within the bounds of discretion). This is seen as a possibility also for Washington's disciples, as the graduates of Tuskegee are represented. "Wherever our graduates go," he writes near the end of his book, "the changes which soon begin to appear in the buying of land, improving homes, saving money, in education, and in high moral character are remarkable. Whole communities are fast being revolutionized through the instrumentality of these men and women" (*US*, 202). The same cannot be said of the masses of blacks who have not been to Tuskegee or who have not come under the Tuskegee influence in some other way. In *Up from Slavery*, they remain blanks. This was hardly the first slave narrative in which the central character saw great distance between himself and other blacks. In Du Bois's *The Souls of Black Folk*, however, that distance would shrink dramatically.

When *The Souls of Black Folk* appeared in 1903, slavery had been officially dead in the United States for forty years. Du Bois himself, thirty-five years of age in 1903, had not been born a slave. Indeed, he had been born on free soil, in Great Barrington, Massachusetts, in a family that had lived there for several generations. One ancestor had even been a revolutionary soldier. Nevertheless, the shadow of slavery hangs powerfully over *The Souls of Black Folk*. Thus Du Bois acknowledged the fact that his book is about a people whose number included many who had been born slaves, and a vast majority who were immediately descended from slaves. On this central point, *The Souls of Black Folk* is a stark contrast to *Up from Slavery*.

In July 1901, shortly after the latter appeared, Du Bois reviewed it in *Dial* magazine. This was his first open criticism of Washington. In 1895, he had saluted Washington's compromising Atlanta Exposition speech as "a word fitly spoken."[8] In the following years, however, he had watched with increasing dismay as the head of Tuskegee propagated his doctrine of compromise and silenced much of his opposition through his manipulation of elements of the black press and other sources of power. Du Bois's attack on him in *Dial* was decisive. The *Dial* review, followed by *The Souls of Black Folk* (where the review again appeared, in adapted form), created "a split of the race into two contending camps," as James Weldon Johnson later noted astutely.[9] Cryptically noting that Washington had given "but glimpses of the real struggle which he has had for leadership," Du Bois accused him of peddling a "Lie."[10] Surveying the various modes of black response to white power from the earliest days in America, he concluded that the vaunted Tuskegee philosophy for black self-improvement was little more than "the old [black] attitude of adjustment to environment, emphasizing the economic phase."

In *The Souls of Black Folk*, unable to fashion an autobiography to match Washington's, young Du Bois nevertheless infused a powerful autobiographical spirit and presence into his essays. From about three dozen of his published articles on aspects of black history and sociology, he selected eight for adaptation or reprinting as nine chapters in *The Souls of Black Folk*. The brief fifth chapter, "Of the Wings of Atalanta," about commercialism and the city of Atlanta, was new, as were the last four chapters: "Of the Passing of the First-Born," Du Bois's prose elegy on the death of his only son, Burghardt; "Of Alexander Crummell," his tribute to an exceptional black man; "Of the Coming of John," a short story; and "Of the Sorrow Songs," an essay on spirituals. Holding these various efforts together is the central figure of Du Bois, who presents himself as a scholar and historian but more dramatically as an artist and a visionary who would not only depict the present state of black culture but also try to prophesy something about its future and the future of the nation.

Du Bois understood clearly that the representation of slavery was central to the entire task. Unlike Washington in *Up from Slavery*, he believed that slavery had been a force of extraordinary—and mainly destructive—potency. Destructive as it had been, however, slavery had not destroyed every major aspect of the African character and psychology (topics on which Washington had been silent); the African core had survived. But so had slavery. Where Washington saw opportunity on every hand for the black, if the right course was followed, Du Bois proclaimed that American slavery was not dead. In one guise or another, it still persisted, with its power scarcely diminished. The act of emancipation had been both a fact (such as Washington loved to fasten on) and a mirage: "Years have passed since then—ten, twenty, forty; forty years of national life, forty years of renewal and development, and yet the swarthy spectre sits in its accustomed seat at the Nation's feast. . . . The Nation has not yet found peace from its sins; the freedman has not yet found in freedom his promised land."[11]

Although there were elements of agreement between Washington and Du Bois on the nature of slavery, *The Souls of Black Folk* portrays the institution in terms essentially opposite to those in *Up from Slavery*. Du Bois does not deny that slavery had its benign side, but in almost every instance his conclusion about its effects is radical when compared with Washington's. American slavery had not been the "worst slavery in the world," and had known something of "kindliness, fidelity, and happiness"; nevertheless, it "classed the black man and the ox together" (*SBF*, 231). Less equivocally, and more typical of Du Bois's view of slavery, black men were "emasculated" by the institution. Emancipation brought them "suddenly, violently . . . into a new birthright" (*SBF*, 227). The white southern universities had been contaminated by "the foul breath of slavery" (*SBF*, 269). Instead of the providential view of slavery espoused by Washington, for Du Bois the institution had amounted to "two hundred and fifty years of assiduous education in submission, carelessness, and stealing" (*SBF*, 323).

Du Bois's emphasis on slavery as a social evil is only one part of the scheme by which he measures the Afro-American and American reality. Central to his argument is his belief in the persistence of the power of slavery beyond emancipation. Many current ills had their start in slavery. The widespread tendency of white businessmen and industrialists to see human beings as property, or "among the material resources of a land to be trained with an eye single to future dividend," was "born of slavery" (*SBF*, 274). The "plague-spot in sexual relations" among blacks—easy marriage and easy separation—"is the plain heritage from slavery" (*SBF*, 306). Many whites in the South live "haunted by the ghost of an untrue dream" (*SBF*, 262). "Slavery and race-prejudice are potent if not sufficient causes of the Negro's position" today (*SBF*, 251). Du Bois does not pretend, in the manner of a demogogue, that slavery and neo-slavery are absolutely identical. He sometimes proposes a new slavery as only a distinct possibility. The power of the ballot, downplayed by Booker T. Washington, is absolutely needed—"else what shall save us from a second slavery?" (*SBF*, 220). And yet, if the black man is not actually a slave, he is actually not free. "Despite compromise, war, and struggle," Du Bois insists, "the Negro is not free" (*SBF*, 239) and is in danger "of being reduced to semi-slavery" (*SBF*, 250). Repeatedly he invokes the central symbol of enslavement to portray the status of the modern black. Today, blacks are "shackled men" (*SBF*, 272).

In the final analysis, black Americans live in neo-slavery. The race passed from formal slavery through an interim illusion of emancipation ("after the first flush of freedom wore off") into a new version of slavery that in many respects continues the old (*SBF*, 308–309). The law courts were used by the white South as the first means of "reenslaving the blacks" (*SBF*, 330). Examining estates that once were slave plantations, Du Bois marvels at how the design and disposition of the black cabins are "the same as in slavery days" (*SBF*, 303). While for Booker T. Washington the Tuskegee education eradicates the vestiges of slavery from students at the institute, Du Bois sees the legacy of slavery as inescapable: "No people a generation removed from slavery can escape a certain unpleasant rawness and *gaucherie*, despite the best of training" (*SBF*, 280). Even the Tuskegee philosophy, as has been pointed out, reflects for Du Bois, in its spirit of compromise, the timidity forced on blacks by slavery.

It is vital to recognize that, far from being the result of distorting bitterness or propaganda, Du Bois's position on neo-slavery at the turn of the century, which he amply documents with vivid examples (many drawn from his personal experience), is fully supported by a wide range of leading historians. Central to their analysis were not simply the repressive local laws but the even more confining decisions of the Supreme Court in *Plessy* v. *Ferguson* in 1896, which held that "separate but equal" facilities were constitutionally valid, and in

Williams v. *Mississippi* in 1898, which endorsed that state's plan to strip blacks of the franchise given them after the Civil War. Rayford W. Logan dubbed the period before the end of the century the "Nadir" of the Afro-American experience.[12] "When complete," C. Vann Woodward wrote of these segregationist laws, "the new codes of White Supremacy were vastly more complex than the ante-bellum slave codes or the Black Codes of 1865–66, and, if anything, they were stronger and more rigidly enforced."[13]

Du Bois's attitude toward slavery, the black present, and the black future is heavily dependent on his attitude toward the preslavery situation of blacks—that is, to Africa. In *The Souls of Black Folk* he does not dwell on the historical evidence of African civilization before slavery that twelve years later would form virtually the main subject of his Pan-Africanist volume, *The Negro* (1915). But where Washington writes only of heathenistic darkness in *Up from Slavery*, Du Bois concedes heathenism but also attributes to the slave a complex, dignified, and usable past. "He was brought from a definite social environment," Du Bois explains,"—the polygamous clan life under the headship of the chief and the potent influence of the priest. His religion was nature-worship, with profound belief in invisible surrounding influences, good and bad, and his worship was through incantation and sacrifice" (*SBF,* 341). In other words, the African lived in a stable, consistent, complex social order, complemented by strong and formal religious beliefs. Far from being a blank, the mind of the black, both in Africa and as a slave brought to the New World, was a remarkable instrument. And because of this background, the slave's natural reaction to slavery was not passivity—which was learned later—but revolt. "Endowed with a rich tropical imagination," Du Bois asserts, "and a keen, delicate appreciation of Nature, the transplanted African lived in a world animate with gods and devils, elves and witches; full of strange influences,—of Good to be implored, of Evil to be propitiated. Slavery, then, was to him the dark triumph of Evil over him. All the fateful powers of the Underworld were striving against him, and a spirit of revolt and revenge filled his heart" (*SBF,* 343).

In ascribing to the black in Africa and in the New World a mind that in its own way is as powerful as that of any other race in the world, Du Bois does more than merely try to boost his race's reputation. He shifts the terms of the debate toward the question of the black mind and character, and introduces questions of history, psychology, myth, and art. He also introduces into his scheme at least two other elements severely downplayed by Washington in *Up from Slavery*. One is the role of imagination; the other, that of memory. Otherwise derogatory of blacks, many white racial "scientists," including the Count de Gobineau, the author of the influential *Essay on the Inequality of Human Races*, had often credited them with remarkable imaginative and artistic faculties (the "rich tropical imagination" Du Bois ascribed to the transplanted African). Du Bois allows this credit to influence not only what he wrote about blacks but also how he wrote it.

Booker T. Washington, finding little that is useful in the African and the slave past, seems in *Up from Slavery* to harbor a deep suspicion of the black imagination, or even to be unaware that it exists. Indeed, his entire attitude toward the imagination contrasts with Du Bois's. While he reads books, or advocates the reading of books, he mentions no novels or poems. He is proud of the fact that his keenest pleasures are in the practical world. "Few things are more satisfactory to me than a high-grade Berkshire or Poland China pig," he writes. "Games I care little for" (*US*, 174). Du Bois is different. From early in his life, he tells us, he has seen the development of his imagination as one possible key to simultaneous self-realization and the leadership of his race against the whites. "Just how I would do it I could never decide," he writes of his youthful dreams of racial and personal victory; "by reading law, by healing the sick, by telling the wonderful tales that swam in my head,—some way" (*SBF*, 214).

In fact, Du Bois's greatest cultural claims for blacks are in the areas of art and imagination. In these claims, slaves play the decisive role. He lauds them as musicians, especially when music is blended with spirituality in the "sorrow songs." In a nation where "vigor and ingenuity" are prized, rather than beauty, "the Negro folk-song—the rhythmic cry of the slave—stands to-day not simply as the sole American music, but as the most beautiful expression of human experience born this side the seas" (*SBF*, 378). Of the three gifts from blacks to American culture, the first is "a gift of story and song—soft, stirring melody in an ill-harmonized and unmelodious land" (*SBF*, 386). (The other gifts are toil and "a gift of the Spirit.")

Recognizing imagination as a source of black strength, and confirming the power of the imagination in Africa, slavery, and thereafter, also freed Du Bois as a thinker and a writer. In his previous book, *The Philadelphia Negro*, he had warned fastidiously that the scholar "must ever tremble lest some personal bias, some moral conviction or some unconscious trend of thought due to previous training, has to a degree distorted the picture in his view."[14] This timidity is abandoned in *The Souls of Black Folk*, which is full of impressionistic writing, including occasionally startling descriptions of people and places, and clearly subjective judgments. Du Bois based the book on his scholarly knowledge of history and sociology, but the eye and mind of the artist are given almost free play.

He was well aware of the possible price of indulging the imagination and even believed that he had paid a part of that price. A year after the book appeared, in a note about it published in the *Independent*, Du Bois conceded that "the style and workmanship" of *The Souls of Black Folk* did not make its meaning "altogether clear."[15] He was sure that the book presented a "clear central message," but also that around this core floated what he called a shadowy "penumbra" of vagueness and partly obscured allusions. Similarly, in his preface, "The Forethought," Du Bois was restrained in outlining his plans. He will sketch, "in vague, uncertain outline," the spiritual world in which the ten million black Americans live (*SBF*, 209). In both pieces, Du Bois is acknowledging the "tropic imagination" of blacks, of which he is one. His elite, formal, Western education has curbed this tropic imagination for too long; now it is free.

A crucial factor here is the connection thus proclaimed between the author of *The Souls of Black Folk* and the masses of American blacks, the despised slaves they had been or were descended from, and the Africans beyond the seas. Du Bois made this connection for all to see when he said of his book, in the note in the *Independent* just cited, that "in its larger aspects the style is tropical—African."[16] In his "Forethought," too, he had linked himself to other blacks, and to slaves: "Need I add that I who speak here am bone of the bone and flesh of the flesh of them that live within the Veil?" (*SBF*, 209).

By indulging his imagination, Du Bois gains for his book much of its distinction. Where Booker T. Washington stresses cold facts, and avoids metaphors and similes, imagination leads Du Bois to the invocation of keen images to represent black reality, and to major insights. Chief among the images is that of "the Veil," which hangs between the black and white races, an apparently harmless fabric but one that the rest of the book shows to be in some respects an almost impregnable wall, and the prime source of misery. In one place he even links his image of the veil to the symbol of an ongoing slavery; at one and the same time, he records "the wail of prisoned souls within the veil, and the mounting fury of shackled men" (*SBF*, 272). Linked to the image of the veil, but going beyond it, and inscribed in the very title of the book, is the idea of black American "double consciousness" (*SBF*, 215). Taking the basic idea of double consciousness as a feature or a capability of the human brain from the reflections of leading psychologists of the time, such as his former professor William James, Du Bois applied the notion with telling force to the mental consequences of the social, political, and cultural conflicts that came with being Afro-American. Perhaps no more challenging single statement about the nature of the black American mind, about the psychological consequences of slavery and racism, has ever been offered. Both the notion of black invisibility and of innately conflicted Afro-American consciousness would be reflected powerfully in future black poetry and fiction.

The "souls" of the title is a play on words. It alludes to the "twoness" of the black American that Du Bois initially suggests in his first chapter. America, a predominantly white country, yields the black "no true self-consciousness, but only lets him see himself through the revelation of the other world" (*SBF*, 214-15). The result is "a peculiar sensation, this double-consciousness, this sense of always looking at one's self through the eyes of others, of measuring one's soul by the tape of a world that looks on in amused contempt and pity. One ever feels his twoness,—an American, a Negro; two souls, two thoughts, two unreconciled strivings; two warring ideals in one dark body, whose dogged strength alone keeps it from being torn asunder" (*SBF*, 215). "Such a double life," Du Bois writes later, in his chapter on religion, "with double thoughts, double duties, and double social classes, must give rise to double words and double ideals, and tempt the mind to pretence or revolt, to hypocrisy or radicalism" (*SBF*, 346). Another way of seeing these two souls surely is as a contest between memory and its opposite, amnesia. American culture demands of its blacks amnesia concerning slavery and Africa, just as it encourages amnesia of a different kind in whites. For Du Bois, blacks may not be able to remember Africa but they should remember slavery, since it has hardly ended.

"In the days of bondage," he writes of the slaves, stressing their imagination, "they thought to see in one divine event the end of all doubt and disappointment; few men ever worshipped Freedom with half such unquestioning faith as did the American Negro for two centuries. . . . In song and exhortation swelled one refrain—Liberty; in his tears and curses the God he implored had Freedom in his right hand. At last it came,—suddenly, fearfully, like a dream" (*SBF*, 216). The first decade after the war "was merely a prolongation of the vain search for freedom, the boon that seemed ever barely to elude their grasp,—like a tantalizing will-o'-the-wisp, maddening and misleading the helpless host" (*SBF*, 217). Freedom never came, but something else did, very faintly, that "changed the child of Emancipation to the youth with dawning self-consciousness, self-realization, self-respect" (*SBF*, 218).

The fundamental progression of the Afro-American in history, as seen by Du Bois, is from a simple bondage to a more complex bondage slightly ameliorated by this "dawning" of "self-consciousness, self-realization, self-respect." "In those sombre forests of his striving, his own soul rose before him, and he saw himself,—darkly as through a veil; and yet he saw in himself some faint revelation of his power, of his mission" (*SBF*, 218). This realization, although "faint," facilitates Du Bois's shift toward what one might call cultural nationalism in the black: "He began to have a dim feeling that, to attain his place in the world, he must be himself, and not another." Cultural nationalism does not mean anti-intellectualism: "For the first time he sought to analyze the burden he bore upon his back, that deadweight of social degradation partially masked behind a half-named Negro problem."

The diminution of the myth of freedom, the elevation of the power of slavery, allows Du Bois to establish a continuum of African and Afro-American psychology. Times change and the nature and amount of data change, but the black mind remains more or less constant, for Du Bois sees it as irrevocably linked to its African origins. If that constancy is anywhere observable, it is for Du Bois in black Christian religion, which in the main is a product of slavery. For him, "the frenzy of a Negro revival in the untouched backwoods of the South" re-creates tellingly "the religious feeling of the slave" (*SBF*, 338). The full meaning of slavery "to the African savage" is unknown to Du Bois, but he believes that the answer is to be found only in "a study of Negro religion as a development" from heathenism to the institutionalized urban churches of the North (*SBF*, 339). The black church is the key to knowing "the inner ethical life of the people who compose it" (*SBF*, 343). Then follows a venture in analysis that may be taken as the foundation of Du Bois's sense of the Afro-American mind, or soul.

By the 1750s, after the initial impulse to revolt had been crushed by white power, "the black slave had sunk, with hushed murmurs, to his place at the bottom of a new economic system, and was unconsciously ripe for a new philosophy of life" (*SBF*, 344). The Christian doctrine of passive submission facilitated this shift in which "courtesy became humility, moral strength degenerated into submission, and the exquisite native appreciation of the beautiful became an infinite capacity for dumb suffering." A century later, black religion had transformed itself once again, this time around the cry for abolition, which became a "religion to the black world. Thus, when Emancipation finally came, it seemed to the freedman a literal Coming of the

Lord. His fervid imagination was stirred as never before, by the tramp of armies, the blood and dust of battle, and the wail and whirl of social upheaval" (*SBF*, 345). Forty years later, with the world changing swiftly, Du Bois sees "a time of intense ethical ferment, of religious heart-searching and intellectual unrest." This leads him, looking backward and forward, into history and into the future. "From the double life every American Negro must live, as a Negro and as an American, as swept on by the current of the nineteenth while yet struggling in the eddies of the fifteenth century,—from this must arise a painful self-consciousness, an almost morbid sense of personality and a moral hesitancy which is fatal to self-confidence" (*SBF*, 346). These are the secondary, but almost equally binding, shackles of neo-slavery.

The authenticity of slavery as metaphor for the black experience is firmly underscored in the most "creative," or imaginative, areas of *The Souls of Black Folk* These are the autobiographical passages of the book; the biographical chapter, on Alexander Crummell; and the short story, "Of the Coming of John." The sharpest focus of the autobiographical element occurs in "Of the Passing of the First-Born," about the death of Du Bois's son (who died of dysentery in Atlanta). In certain respects this is an almost classical elegy, in impassioned and yet formal language. But it is one in which the central mourner, as a black, can find no consolation. Thus it is in truth anti-Christian, a bitter parody of the Christian elegy such as Milton's *Lycidas*. For Du Bois, unable to believe in Booker T. Washington's Providence, doubt completely infects his vision of his son's future: "If still he be, and he be There, and there be a There, let him be happy, O Fate!" (*SBF*, 352). Perhaps one day the veil will be lifted and the imprisoned blacks set free, but not in Du Bois's time: "Not for me,—I shall die in my bonds" (*SBF*, 353). The metaphor of black life as slavery preempts the annealing possibilities of the elegy.

This chapter underscores the memorable autobiographical impressions left by the first few pages of the book, in which Du Bois discusses his first, youthful encounter with racism: "Then it dawned upon me with a certain suddenness that I was different from the others [his white classmates]; or like, mayhap, in heart and life and longing, but shut out from their world by a vast veil" (*SBF*, 214). Taking refuge in fierce competitiveness, he wins small victories but understands at last that "the worlds I longed for, and all their dazzling opportunities, were theirs, not mine." Many of his black friends deteriorate into sycophancy or into hatred and distrust of whites. Du Bois does not, but "the shades of the prison-house closed round about us all; walls strait and stubborn to the whitest, but relentlessly narrow, tall, and unscalable to sons of night."

Thus, just as the acceptance of the idea of neo-slavery forbids Du Bois the writing of classical elegy, with its formal consolation, so does that acceptance also forbid Du Bois the writing of anything that resembles either the "classical" slave narrative—the account of a life that has passed from bondage to freedom, from darkness to light—or its white American counterpart, the rags-to-riches autobiographical tale built on the materialist base of the American Dream. Indeed, if one isolates Du Bois as the hero of *The Souls of Black Folk*, one sees the reverse pattern. He goes from light into darkness, from the freedom of infancy and childhood into the bondage of maturity. Each modern black American, he argues implicitly, re-creates this regressive journey. So too has the black race, in its New World experience, enacted a historical regression. Preslavery African manhood and womanhood have deteriorated into passivity, moral hesitancy, cynicism, and rage.

Du Bois does not see all blacks as succumbing to pressure, but in any event those who resist have no hope of a lasting triumph. The most honored single figure in *The Souls of Black Folk* is Alexander Crummell (1819–1898), who struggled against tremendous odds but succeeded in being ordained as a priest in the almost entirely white Protestant Episcopal Church, earned a degree from Cambridge University, then went on to years of diligent service in Africa and the United States. Crummell also helped to found the American Negro Academy, in which Du Bois himself was involved. Clearly he stands as Du Bois's idea of the highest achievement among black Americans. Pointedly, Crummell was born when "the slave-ship still groaned across the Atlantic" (*SBF*, 355). His life is one of trial and tribulation, but also of resistance to doubt, hatred, and despair. He decides early to live for his people: "He heard the hateful clank of their chains; he felt them cringe and grovel, and there rose within him a protest and a prophesy" (*SBF*, 357). But no great triumph followed. For all his service and achievement, Crummell's name is now barely known. "And herein lies the tragedy of the age: not that men are poor,—all men know something of poverty; not that men are wicked,—who is good? not that men are ignorant,—what is Truth? Nay, but that men know so little of men" (*SBF*, 362). Again, the consolation of faith is impossible: "I wonder where he is today?"

The short story "Of the Coming of John" (in a sense, one of "the wonderful tales that swam in my head" to which Du Bois alludes early in the book) further underscores the destructive force of neo-slavery (*SBF*, 214). Black John, a simple country boy, comes to "Wells Institute" to be educated. But education cannot save him from racism, and his spirit deteriorates: "A tinge of sarcasm crept into his speech, and a vague bitterness into his life" (*SBF*, 367). Education alienates him from his own people; he returns home only to be struck by the "sordidness and narrowness" of what he had left behind (*SBF*, 370). Unwittingly he tramples on the religious beliefs of the local blacks, and he preaches democracy in the black school although it is under the control of a reactionary white judge. Dismissed from his job there, he wanders in a daze until he sees his sister tussling with a white man he had known as a boy. He kills the man. John tells his mother he is is going away—"I'm going to be free" (*SBF*, 376). Not understanding, she asks if he is going north again. "Yes, mammy," John replies, "I'm going,—North." He is soon lynched by revengeful whites. Going north and freedom are meaningless for John and for blacks in America. Freedom does not exist, except in death.

Education is only one of the forces that, subverted by racism and neo-slavery, betray John when he should have been elevated by them. For a person of Du Bois's complicated and elite schooling, this must have been a particularly poignant aspect to the condition he describes. Education should lead to light and truth. Booker T. Washington rearranged the chronology of his life in *Up from Slavery* to end his book close to the dizzying personal height of a Harvard honorary degree awarded in 1896 to the former illiterate slave. With the invitation in hand, "tears came into my eyes" (*US*, 190). But education for John leads to darkness and death. The fate of Alexander Crummell and of the author of *The Souls of Black Folk* is not much more exalted.

The Souls of Black Folk offers no transcendent confidence in the future. Du Bois's essay on religion, "Of the Faith of the Fathers," ends with an assertion of the existence of "the deep religious feeling of the real Negro heart, the stirring, unguided might of powerful human souls who have lost the guiding star of the past and seek in the great night a new religious ideal" (*SBF*, 349). Only in concluding the book does Du Bois appeal to the longest possible historical view. The assumption of whites that certain races cannot be "saved" is "the arrogance of people irreverent toward Time and ignorant of the deeds of men. A thousand years ago such an assumption, easily possible, would have made it difficult for the Teuton to prove his right to life" (*SBF*, 386). As powerful as it was, American slavery thus becomes for him, in the end, only an episode in the African people's history, not the history itself.

Before this point, however, he has engaged slavery valiantly in his text. His point of view is clear. Admitting and exploring the reality of slavery is necessarily painful for a black American, but only by doing so can he or she begin to understand himself or herself and American and Afro-American culture in general. The normal price of the evasion of the fact of slavery is intellectual and spiritual death. Only by grappling with the meaning and legacy of slavery can the imagination, recognizing finally the temporality of the institution, begin to transcend it.

NOTES

1. Benjamin Brawley, *The Negro in Literature and Art* (New York: Duffield, 1918), 18.

2. James Weldon Johnson, *Along This Way* (New York: Viking, 1968), 203.

3. John Henrik Clarke, Esther Jackson, Ernest Kaiser, and J. H. O'Dell,

eds., *Black Titan: W. E. B. Du Bois: An Anthology by the Editors of Freedomways* (Boston: Beacon Press, 1970), 8.

4. W. E. B. Du Bois, *The Souls of Black Folk*, ed. J. Saunders Redding (New York: Fawcett, 1961), ix.

5. Herbert Aptheker, *Annotated Bibliography of the Published Writings of W. E. B. Du Bois* (Millwood, N.Y.: Kraus-Thomson, 1973), 551.

6. Henry James, *The American Scene* (Bloomington: University of Indiana Press, 1960), 418.

7. Booker T. Washington, *Up from Slavery*, in *Three Negro Classics* (New York: Avon, 1965), 37. Subsequent parenthetical references in the text are to this edition; hereafter abbreviated as *US*.

8. Herbert Aptheker, ed., *Selections; 1877–1934*; vol. 1 of *The Correspondence of W. E. B. Du Bois* (Amherst: University of Massachusetts Press, 1973), 39.

9. James Weldon Johnson, *Black Manhattan* (New York: Knopf, 1930), 134.

10. W. E. B. Du Bois, "The Evolution of Negro Leadership," *Dial* 31 (July 16, 1901): 53–55.

11. W. E. B. Du Bois, *The Souls of Black Folk*, in *Three Negro Classics*, 216. Subsequent parenthetical references in the text are to this edition; hereafter abbreviated as *SBF*.

12. See Rayford W. Logan, *The Negro in American Life and Thought: The Nadir, 1877–1901* (New York: Dial, 1954).

13. C. Vann Woodward, *Origins of the New South, 1877–1913* (Baton Rouge: Louisiana State University Press, 1951), 212.

14. W. E. B. Du Bois, *The Philadelphia Negro: A Social Study* (Philadelphia, 1899), 3.

15. W. E. B. Du Bois, "The Souls of Black Folk," *Independent* 57 (November 17, 1904): 1152.

16. Ibid.

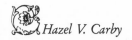 Hazel V. Carby

Ideologies of Black Folk

THE HISTORICAL NOVEL OF SLAVERY

The title "Slavery and the Literary Imagination" should generate reflection on the ways in which we, as literary critics, have constructed Afro-American literary history. Slavery appears to be central to the Afro-American literary imagination, but, as a mode of production and as a particular social order, slavery is rarely the focus of the imaginative physical and geographical terrain of Afro-American novels. The occasion for this essay is, therefore, a paradox.

One might explain this paradox in three ways. First, there is the critical influence on Afro-American literary history of the antebellum slave narrative. Henry Louis Gates, Jr., has argued in *The Slave's Narrative* that slave narratives have had a determining influence on Afro-American literature. Gates's theoretical proposition is that critical practice needs to elaborate a "black intertextual or signifying relationship" in order to produce "any meaningful formal literary history of the Afro-American tradition."[1] Narrative strategies repeated through two centuries of black writing are seen as the link that binds the slave narrative to texts as disparate as Booker T. Washington's *Up From Slavery*, *The Autobiography of Malcolm X.*, Ralph Ellison's *Invisible Man*, Richard Wright's *Black Boy*, *Their Eyes Were Watching God* by Zora Neale Hurston, and *Flight to Canada* by Ishmael Reed. As readers and as writers, then, we become receivers of a textual experience that creates the unity of an Afro-American literary tradition, a tradition that, Gates concludes, "rests on the framework built, by fits and starts and for essentially polemical intentions, by the first-person narratives of black ex-slaves."[2] Contemporary Afro-American literary discourse thus situates a form of cultural production that reconstructs the social conditions of slavery as the basis of the entire narrative tradition.

Second, slavery haunts the literary imagination because its material conditions and social relations are frequently reproduced in fiction as historically dynamic; they continue to influence society long after emancipation. The economic and social system of slavery is thus a prehistory (as well as a pre-text to all Afro-American texts), a past social condition that can explain contemporary phenomena. In the late nineteenth century the novels of Frances E. W. Harper, Pauline Hopkins, and Charles Chesnutt used slavery in this sense. For example, Hopkins's *Contending Forces* (1900) begins with an eighty-page slave story that acts as an overture to her tale of a black New England family at the turn of the century.[3] Her slave prehistory provides all the necessary elements for the fictional resolutions to the novel; once Hopkins's characters *know* their history, they can control their futures. In a formal sense slavery can thus be a most powerful "absent" presence, and this device was perhaps most effectively used by W. E. B. Du Bois in *The Souls of Black Folk*, in which the slave condition, if not the slave mode of production, permeates the text.[4]

Third, our ideas of an Afro-American literary tradition are dominated by an ideology of the "folk" from fictional representations of sharecropping. These novels, which might be called "novels of sharecropping," are those texts, central to contemporary reconstructions of an Afro-American canon, which are interpreted as representations of the Southern "folk"—a folk emerging from and still influenced by the slave condition. Indeed, I would argue that the critical project that situates the ex-slaves writing their "selfhood" or their "humanity" into being as the source of Afro-American literature also reconstructs black culture as rooted in a "folk" culture. The ex-slave consciousness becomes an original "folk" consciousness. Critics like Gates and Houston A. Baker, Jr., argue that the means of expression of this consciousness is the vernacular—for Baker it is the blues that is the "always already" of Afro-American culture—and the search for this vernacular structures and informs the intellectual projects of both critics. Intertextuality is the concept that makes the abstract theoretical proposition a material relation, which is characterized as a series of variations, or riffs, on an original theme to produce an Afro-American discourse, or "blues matrix."[5]

But in the production of this discourse the critical vernacular itself dissolves historical difference. A mythology of the rural South conflates the nineteenth and twentieth centuries and two very distinct modes of production, slavery and sharecropping, into one mythical rural folk existence. Of course, the ideological function of a tradition is to create unity out of disunity and to resolve the social contradiction, or differences, between texts. Consequently, not only are the specificities of a slave existence as opposed to a sharecropping existence negated, but the urban imagination and urban histories are also repressed. Our twentieth-century vernacular (the blues, if you like) is reinterpreted as emerging from a shared rural heritage, not as the product of social displacement and migration to the city. The fact that imaginative recreations of the "folk" including the ex-slave, are themselves produced and distributed primarily within the urban environment and for urban consumption is not critically examined. A few examples of general critical trends will suffice to illustrate the dominance of this concern with the "folk."

In Zora Neale Hurston's *Their Eyes Were Watching God*, the character of Janie seeks to establish her independence and selfhood by breaking away from the limited possibilities for female existence imagined by her grandmother, a woman shaped by the slave condition.[6] Hurston's highly romanticized novel is read by many contemporary critics as the epitome of "folk" wisdom; one might recall that this representation of the "folk" was decried as "minstrelsy" by Richard Wright, Langston Hughes, and Arna Bontemps, and condemned as being a result of Hurston's reactionary politics.[7] On the other hand, there is little critical assessment of the ways in which Richard Wright attempted to rewrite and restructure representations of the rural folk in terms influenced by proletarian fiction and his radical political commitments. And, finally, a large proportion of the criticism written about Ralph Ellison's *Invisible Man* focuses on a minor section of the text, the "Trueblood" episode, a representation of a "folk" figure that covers 20 pages out of a novel of 568 pages, most of which is set in an urban context. It is these 20 pages that Baker analyzes, for example, in his critical search for the vernacular tradition in *Blues, Ideology, and Afro-American Literature*.[8]

These romantic evocations of the Afro-American folk motif are to be felt not only in Afro-American critical work but, at the moment, dominate the few representations of the black community in mass American culture. A romanticized folk has recently been reproduced by the entertainment industry in the movie *The Color Purple*. It is a sobering thought that perhaps Steven Spielberg's film is as romanticized a response to black culture in the eighties as David Selznick's *Gone With the Wind* was to black culture in the thirties.

The results of this conflation of slavery and sharecropping into a rural folk that is at the base of the creation of an Afro-American canon is, however, another essay. The idea that the ex-slaves "wrote [their selves] into being" through an account of the condition of being a slave is woven into the very fabric of the Afro-American literary imagination and its critical reconstruction. However, novelistic representations of slavery are critically neglected, and why this is so intrigues me. This essay will look at this minority tendency in Afro-American literature, the historical novel of slavery, and in particular at Arna Bontemps's *Black Thunder* and Margaret Walker's *Jubilee*.[9] These texts have received little critical attention, but what interests me the most about these historical novels is the choice of slavery as a period in which to set historical fiction and how that choice itself is generated from particular cultural conditions. I want to distinguish my critical position from a preoccupation with a historically undifferentiated "folk," and I hope to reinsert a concern with history both at the level of formal analysis and in relation to the moment of cultural production.

I want to outline a number of different ways of thinking about the relation between history and historical fiction, but first I should state some general principles. As Warren Susman has argued, myth, memory, and history are three alternative ways to capture and account for an allusive past. Each has its own persuasive claim.[10] I am going to concentrate upon the two latter approaches, memory and history, first by looking at the novel of memory and oral culture– curiously, both Walker's *Jubilee* and Margaret Mitchell's *Gone with the Wind*.[11] Then I will look at the novel of slave rebellion, *Black Thunder*, and its cultural context. Each represents particular ideologies of the folk which are shaped by the cultural context in which they are produced.

Margaret Walker's *Jubilee* has been heralded as a reaffirmation of "the critical importance of oral tradition in the creation of [Afro-American] history" in a "work based on black memories."[12] Published in 1966, *Jubilee* was a novel that seemed to engage directly the concerns of the civil rights movement and the ideologies of the new Black Aesthetic. Its revisionist history, which utilized Afro-American oral culture as well as years of painstaking research, was seen by the Institute for the Black World, which published Walker's essay *"How I Wrote Jubilee,"* as an important contribution to the "challenge to the White Western value system — especially in education."[13] Walker herself has emphasized that she drew upon family history, that throughout her childhood she heard "stories of slave life in Georgia" from her grandmother, who retold incidents from her mother's life. *Jubilee*, Walker maintains, is the result of a promise to her grandmother that she would write her mother's story.[14] The paperback cover calls Vyry, the protagonist, "a heroine to rival Scarlett O'Hara" and proclaims the "devastating truth" of the story as it is "steeped in knowledge of and feeling for . . . the people." The relation of oral history to the production of the fictional world was seen to be important not only in a general sense that it was history from the bottom up, the "people's version," but also as a particular response to the dominant ideologies of the popular imagination embodied in Mitchell's *Gone with the Wind*.

The recovery of an Afro-American history embedded in an oral culture has formed a very important part of the challenge to dominant interpretations of American history. But in the twenties Margaret Mitchell also felt that she was writing a revisionist history, the story of the beaten but undefeated South. Like Walker, what she felt authenticated *her* historical "truth" against what she saw to be a dominant Northern version of history was the fact that she was writing from family memories, an oral history retold. Mitchell, too, had spent her formative years listening to stories of her ancestors and can be regarded as being as involved as Walker in the preservation of an oral cul-

ture. In a letter, Mitchell described the relation of this oral history to
Gone with the Wind: "I was writing about an upheaval I'd heard about
when I was a small child. For I spent Sunday afternoons of my childhood sitting on the bony knees of Confederate veterans and the fat
slick laps of old ladies who survived the war and reconstruction."[15]

Both Walker and Mitchell authenticate their texts through references to popular memory, and both could be said to be re-creating cultural meaning through the vernacular of their fictional and historical
subjects. But as Georg Lukacs has argued, history has "not aesthetic,
but social and historical causes." Clearly, *Gone with the Wind* and *Jubilee* express very different historical "truths," particularly about the
slave condition.[16]

Mitchell wrote *Gone with the Wind* in the twenties. Her novel
epitomizes what Susman has characterized as the "fear" that runs
through much writing of the twenties and thirties—the fear "whether
any great industrial and democratic mass society can maintain a significant level of civilization, and whether mass education and mass
communication will allow any civilization to survive."[17] Susman's
argument is that the concept of civilization that in the late-nineteenth
and early-twentieth centuries was synonymous with social advance
and progress became detached from, and indeed opposed to, these
terms to the extent that progress was considered to be at the risk of
the destruction of civilization. In *Gone with the Wind*, a multiplicity
of the cultural meanings of civilization compete with each other. The
figure of Scarlett O'Hara is a representation of this conflict. Mitchell's
landscape is the destruction of one civilization and the possibilities
offered to build another. Scarlett is in many ways the new capitalist
woman who literally builds the new Atlanta, an industrializing city,
with the wood from her own lumberyard. The constant battle against
rigid conventions that govern female behavior rewrites Mitchell's own
unconventional response to ideologies of womanhood in the twenties. In these two important ways *Gone with the Wind* is a text that recognizes the uneasy relationship between elements of progress and
civilization but ultimately confirms a future that must inevitably
bind the two. But for my purposes here what is most important is

that Mitchell's fears of a mass democracy are condensed into her representations of the newly emancipated black folk.

The postwar chapters of *Gone with the Wind* are filled with long passages that describe in horrified terms mass assemblies of black people on the streets of Atlanta. Mitchell represents emancipation as chaos, and blacks uncontrolled by white people as the force with the potential to destroy civilization. What Mitchell describes as the class system that structured black people into house servants and field hands before the war is turned upside down; "the lowest and most ignorant ones were on the top." What Mitchell fears are the "hordes of 'trashy free issue niggers' who like monkeys or small children turned loose among treasured objects ... ran wild." Atlanta's streets are crowded with black people who are "lazy and dangerous"; the refusal to work is a threat to the future prosperity and growth of the city; and uncontrolled black male sexuality, a threat to all white womanhood. If uncontrolled or "free" blacks are the mass threat to civilization, what can preserve civilization is perpetual slavery. Mitchell's black folk figures who are individually characterized are all personal servants devoted to their mistresses. In the antebellum chapters they are of course slaves, but the material conditions of this relation to the white people for whom they work do not change; after emancipation they remain virtually slaves. While most of *Gone with the Wind* is concerned with the representation of massive social upheaval and turmoil—out of the ashes of one civilization has to rise another—both civilizations must be based on an ideology of black people bound to this form of servility. As Mitchell writes, the "better class" of blacks "scorn[ed] freedom," "loyal field hands ... refused to avail themselves of the new freedom," and "abandoned negro children" were taken by "kind-hearted white people ... into their kitchens to raise."[18]

It is crucially important to consider *Gone with the Wind* because as a novel and as a film it has become the dominant mass cultural mythology of the formation of the rural black folk. The novel was published in 1936 and the movie premièred in 1939. The titles that open the film establish the same conditions for black people as the novel:

there are no "slaves" who are named such because all black characters are listed under the headings "The House Servants" and "In the Fields." Yet the film confirms the fact that all the major black characters are slaves, and they remain in the same social position after "emancipation." But the Hollywood version of the tale rewrites Mitchell's vision in some respects. First, there is no forceful presence of massed blacks about to destroy the very basis of civilization. Clearly this is a concession to the growing effectiveness of black pressure groups in the Hollywood of the thirties. Second, there is the presence of Hattie McDaniel. McDaniel's performance is important because she rewrites in terms of visual imaging Mitchell's main literary black folk/slave figure and occasionally breaks through the limits of the cinematic black folk/slave figure written by the Hollywood scriptwriters. Hattie McDaniel contests for the first time in a product of American mass culture the literary source of the archetypal slave figure, the "Mammy." In this respect it is crucial to be aware of the engagement of the literary with a wider cultural imagination, for McDaniel manages to reconstruct for mass consumption a product of the literary imagination.

Near the beginning of the film is a scene that illustrates the possibilities and the limits of McDaniel's contestation of the figure of the "Mammy." In preparation for a ball, Hattie McDaniel dresses a willful Vivian Leigh. Whether "Mammy" can also persuade "Scarlett" to eat before the party and thus preserve the appearance of a birdlike appetite in public, which convention requires of a lady, provides the occasion for a confrontation between them in which the full range of the stereotypical behavior of the "Mammy" figure is mobilized. McDaniel cajoles, bullies, and wheedles. But, at the climactic moment of the scene, the contradiction between the Hollywood construction of the black woman as "Mammy," and McDaniel's performance, is clear. In her face the audience recognizes not only the fictional triumph of "Mammy" over the willful mistress but the triumph of McDaniel as an actress over the limitations of her role. For one brief moment the text cannot contain the implications of McDaniel's expression of complete disdain, and expected filmic and social meanings are disrupted for the spectator. Perhaps the most enduring of the literary conventions of slavery to have emerged from the plantation novels, the "Mammy" figure, becomes in McDaniel's performance a contradictory space through subtle changes of facial expression and body movement. Her performance reveals the ideological contradictions of both Mitchell's ideas of loyal servants who eschew freedom and Selznick's liberal gesture in portraying blacks as peasants rather than as slaves.[19]

Gone with the Wind cements the relation between the literary and filmic imaginations in the twentieth century, and both movie and novel re-create the historical romance of an American slave society. This romanticism, which Lukacs describes as "history transformed into a series of moral lessons for the present," re-creates a mythological slave condition, a carefully controlled space for the black folk in the South that resolves the social conflicts arising from black migration to southern cities and to the North in the twenties and thirties.[20]

Margaret Walker's *Jubilee* is in many ways a direct response to this mythology and to the conditions that allowed the mythology to flourish. Though the original source of her tale was in memories and oral culture, Walker transforms these memories through the structure of the social realist novel. One of the most powerful influences on the formal structure of the text was Lukac's *The Historical Novel*. "I have Lukacs to thank for an understanding of the popular character of the historical novel," she says. Walker uses the analysis of Lukacs to fuse popular memory with her extensive historical research in order to represent the transformations of history as the transformations of popular life.

Walker's social commitment to realism tempers her approach to her folk material. She carefully documented folk sayings, beliefs, songs, and folkways for inclusion in her text, but she deliberately avoids a romantic evocation of an undifferentiated rural folk. All her characters, major and minor, are actors in history and, at the same time, are produced and shaped by that history. Walker's main protagonist, Vyry, is described as a product of plantation life and culture who has been "shaped by the forces that dominated her life," forces that limit her vision of the potential for social change. Randall Ware, the man

Vyry marries, on the other hand, is a militant. Ware believes in the possibility and, indeed, the inevitability of social transformation; as a member of an artisan class of free laborers, he has a limited amount of freedom to travel and therefore to be active in the underground railroad. Vyry wants freedom, but she finds it hard at first to believe in, and then to imagine, its possibilities; Ware determines that escape from the South is a political necessity to continue an effective fight against slavery once civil war seems inevitable. Both see their children as the future. Ware insists that the children must be left behind; Vyry cannot do that, tries to escape with them, and is caught and returned to the plantation for a brutal whipping. Vyry and Ware, permanently separated, come to represent two opposing responses to the Civil War and reconstruction. Because of her particular slave experience Vyry searches for a home that is secure from white terrorists and for work that will make her a valuable resource for a white community and thus secure for her and her children a degree of protection. Ware, more aggressive, is dissatisfied with any compromise on his freedom. But both survive to shape different communal responses to an oppressive white society. Though I have described only two of Walker's folk, their position as the bearers and shapers of history is characteristic of the whole text. Walker's ideology of a black folk forged from the social system of slavery is a fictional representation of Lukacs's formulation of historical necessity. Historical necessity, he argues, "is no other worldly fate divorced from men; it is the complex interaction of concrete historical circumstances in their process of transformation, in their interaction with the concrete human beings, who have grown up in these circumstances, have been variously influenced by them, and who act in an individual way according to personal passions."[21]

Hortense Spillers has characterized *Jubilee* as "theonomous," a novel that is "not only historical but also, and primarily, Historical. . . . a metaphor for the unfolding of the Divine Will." In consequence, Spillers asserts, "agents (or characters) are moving and are moved under the aegis of a Higher and Hidden Authority." The "heroic as transparent prophetic utterance" becomes the "privileged center of human response."

If Walker's characters are ultimately seen as one dimensional, either good or bad, speaking in a public rhetoric that assumes the heroic or its opposite, then such portrayal is apt to a fiction whose value is subsumed in a theonomous frame of moral reference. From this angle of advocacy and preservation the writer does not penetrate the core of experience, but encircles it. The heroic intention has no interest in fluctuations or transformations or palpitations of conscience . . . but monumentality, or fixedness, becomes its striving. Destiny is disclosed to the hero or the heroine as an already-fixed and named event, and this steady reference point is the secret of permanence.

Spillers concludes that the characters "embody historical symbols – a captive class and their captors" and that these symbols have been encoded into actors in a future, making them "types or valences," masks through which they speak. The characters in this "theonomous view of human reality . . . are overdrawn . . . their compelling agency and motivation are ahistorical, despite the novel's solid historical grounding."[22]

These are important criticisms that point to the limits of historical possibility represented in the text, especially in relation to Vyry. Vyry's inability to imagine freedom is compounded by her reluctance to attempt an escape without her children. While she hesitates by her cabin door, her toddler wakes and asks where she is going. Vyry's reply "Nowhere" is not just a mother's reassurance to a child but also foreshadows her abortive attempt to run. Spillers interprets Vyry's journey into the swamp carrying a baby and dragging a toddler as the replication of the "paralysis of nightmare," the articulation of which "dictates the crucial psychological boundaries of *Jubilee* and decides, accordingly, the aesthetic rule."[23]

But Vyry's dilemma is not merely discursive. The psychological and aesthetic boundaries are shaped by two histories, a fictional reconstruction of the eve of the Civil War and the moment of the cultural production of the text. As historical agent, Vyry acts within the conventional parameters of woman as mother. The presence of children in slave narratives made the slave woman's relation to escape more complex than that of slave men.[24] Walker is clearly historicizing the contradiction for slave women between being a "good" mother and being free. However, Spillers's critical charges accurately describe the paucity of imaginative possibilities. As *Jubilee* entered the cultural conditions of 1966, it offered a severely limited historical, psychological, and aesthetic vision of the possibilities of a free black community. Vyry's search for security becomes synonymous with dependence on white patronage.

However, Walker's rewriting of a folk ideology appeared to speak directly to the social transformations of the sixties while, at the same time, it was rooted in her response to the thirties and proletarian literature. Walker's political consciousness was shaped in the thirties when she worked for the WPA and wrote about black migrants to the South Side of Chicago. She worked on a novel about a Chicago ghetto called *Goose Island* for a couple of years, but it was never published.[25] In the many years it took to write *Jubilee* sporadically between the thirties and the sixties Walker remained committed to "showing the interrelationships of class as well as race and . . . how these interrelationships shape the political, economic, and social structure in the entire panorama of the novel."[26] Walker's representation of slavery is her philosophy of history, which is to be understood as the necessary prehistory of contemporary society. The Civil War, she argues, was a bloody revolution, an inevitable and "irrepressible conflict brought on by great economic, political, and social forces of change." The promise of liberty and freedom she views as being defeated by "a white Southern counter-revolution" in which black people remained as pawns, "a sub-culture unrecognized by the dominant culture."[27]

A very different appropriation of slave history was made by Arna Bontemps in *Black Thunder*, published the same year as *Gone with the Wind* (1936) and reprinted in 1968[28] as the American culture industry rediscovered the 1930s. In particular, "the literary marketplace . . . rediscover[ed] novels virtually unread and critically ignored in the period and now hailed as significant."[29] In his 1968 introduction to this fictional reconstruction of the revolt of Gabriel Prosser in Virginia in 1800, Bontemps wonders if a story of "black self-assertion," of "volcanic rumblings among angry blacks," would find a more under-

standing audience after the death of Martin Luther King and after the
Watts rebellion.[30] But if the late sixties appeared ready for the distribution of a literary black revolution, Bontemps wrote *Black Thunder* at
a moment when rebellion against oppression seemed imminent. Two
stories "dominated the news" and the "daydreams of the people" that
he met, he recounts, "the demonstrations of Mahatma Gandhi and his
followers in India and the trials of the Scottsboro boys."[31] In this atmosphere of "bleak hostility" Bontemps visited Fisk University and
discovered "a larger collection of slave narratives than I knew existed."[32] Out of his reading of these slave narratives came *Black
Thunder.*

Bontemps's novel also prefigures Afro-American historiography in
the late sixties and seventies, which would focus on the slave through
slave testimony. What Bontemps calls his "frantic" reading of slave narratives for a historical novel was not the central concern of Afro-
American historians for another thirty years, when a "concern for
demonstrating the nature and strengths of black culture became an
important aspect of research dealing with black America."[33] The
Slave Narrative Collection was compiled by the WPA between 1936
and 1938, but interviews with ex-slaves were collected during the twenties and kept at Fisk, and Bontemps must have read some of them.
The narratives from interviews contain much more of the "informal
folk aspects of [the] daily round of slave life" that, Norman Yetman
has argued, make these narratives very different from the "highly
formalized, even stylized" structure of the antebellum slave narratives
now considered canonic.[34]

Afro-American historians are divided about the merits of using
either the informal interviews or the antebellum narratives. In the sixties, Bontemps edited a collection of the latter, but *Black Thunder* certainly appears to have been influenced by these less formal interviews.
The novel re-creates in the daily round of slave life a black culture that
existed as a space away from the control of whites.

The approach of literary critics to the antebellum narratives has
been rather different from that of the historians. Contemporary
critics see the struggle to attain literacy in the antebellum narratives as

a means of asserting humanity. But in *Black Thunder* Bontemps uses
literacy as a means by which his characters realize the necessity of revolution. "Reading's bad for a nigger. You just reads and you reads and
pretty soon you sees where it say, Brother, come and unite with us
and let us combat for a common good; then you is plum done for.
You ain't no mo' count for bowing and scraping and licking boots.
Oh, it's bad when niggers get to holding out they arms, touching
hands, saying Brother this, Brother that, they is about to meet the
whirlwind then."[35] Bontemps's slave folk are like Richard Wright's rebellious peasantry but they are also represented as having a community and culture that is a source for their group resistance. It was not
until the 1970s that Afro-American historiography applied the same
analysis to the ways in which the black community sustained itself
under the slave system.

The novel is the history of a community of black people inspired by
the successful revolution in San Domingo (Haiti) led by Toussaint
L'Ouverture. A group of both slave and free blacks is represented as
influenced by Jacobinism and, more important, by a reinterpretation
of the Bible by those in the group who can read. "God don't like ugly"
and "God's against them what oppresses the po'" are phrases constantly
repeated throughout the narrative to authenticate the justice of revolutionary action and the right to seek revenge against oppression.

In a review of *Black Thunder*, Richard Wright asserted that the
novel was the only one he knew "dealing forthrightly with the historical and revolutionary traditions of the Negro people," and he praised
Bontemps for the creation of a protagonist who displayed "a quality
of folk courage unparalleled in the proletarian literature of this country."[36] The recovery of revolutionary traditions not only was the concern of proletarian literature but was echoed in black historiography
during the thirties. During this period—the depression decade—the
first substantial studies of slave rebellions were produced. Responding
to black colonial oppression in ways similar to Bontemps's work,
C. L. R. James's epic history *The Black Jacobins* was published in 1938,
and in the following year the first version of Herbert Aptheker's path-
breaking *Negro Slave Revolts* was issued.[37]

James's narrative of the revolution of Toussaint L'Ouverture was written in direct response to representations of people of African descent "constantly being the object of other peoples' exploitation and ferocity." Instead, James portrayed black people "taking action on a grand scale and shaping other people to their own needs."[38] Aptheker's introduction to *Negro Slave Revolts* reflects his awareness of the ways in which historians' re-creations of the past are directly engaged with other cultural representations of history. He wrote to revise a history that was a "wholly erroneous conception of life in the old South" which dominated "movies and novels and textbooks [and was] invented by the slaveholders themselves."[39] Like Aptheker and James, Bontemps made a claim to a revolutionary black tradition that directly opposed the historiography of Ulrich Bonnell Phillips in *Life and Labor in the Old South*, an interpretation of plantation life generally considered to be a definitive history and embodied in Mitchell's *Gone with the Wind*.[40] Like Mitchell, Phillips was a Georgian who also referenced a popular memory of an idyllic South.[41]

In formal terms, a narrative of slavery has three conventional conclusions: escape, emancipation, or death. Antebellum slave narratives conventionally ended with escape to the North. In historical sagas like *Jubilee*, emancipation is central. In novels based on rebellions, death is the conclusion. In three contemporary novels of slavery these conventions are rewritten. In Ishmael Reed's *Flight to Canada*, a postmodernist revision of the antebellum slave narrative and a novelistic representation of intertextuality, the escaped slave, Raven, returns to the plantation from Canada. In Sherley Anne Williams's *Dessa Rose*, slaves escape not to the North but to the West. In perhaps the most interesting revision of the form of the historical novel, David Bradley's *The Chaneysville Incident*, escape leads to death, and death itself is also a form of escape.[42]

Black Thunder opens with the testimony of a planter who recounts the discovery of a planned insurrection of over eleven hundred slaves to the Virginia Court in September 1800, "a testimony that caused half the states to shudder." It concludes with a vision of "Gabriel's shining body [and the] arc inscribed by the executioner's ax." Death awaits not only the revolutionary heroes but also the traitors. Ben Sheppard, a slave who betrays the planned revolution to the authorities, turns from looking at the execution block to the scene of Gabriel's lover being sold on the auction block and knows that in every hedge there are knives waiting for him.[43] Death is not just a risk in the cause of freedom but is preferable to slavery. "'A wild bird what's in a cage will die anyhow, sooner or later,' Gabriel said. 'He'll pine hisself to death. He just is well to break his neck trying to get out.'"[44]

Death, in a narrative of slave rebellion, offers a figure of future revolution. Narratives of escape are usually organized as individual biographies; they are unlike the narratives of sharecropping, which are usually family stories. The historical novel that uses emancipation is bound by history in a particular way—emancipation is final and the narrative has to move on in history. But a narrative of slave rebellion can be read as a figure for the revolutionary change that has not come. James, in the context of colonial politics, and Bontemps, in the context of American oppression, were representing the collective acts of a black community as signs for future collective acts of rebellion and liberation.

The critically neglected novels of Walker and Bontemps challenge ideologies of a romantic rural folk tradition. Both writers worked for the WPA Illinois Project and were closely involved with the migrants who came to form the black urban community in Chicago in the thirties. Walker's poetry in her collection *For My People* and Bontemps's collaboration with Jack Conroy on *They Seek a City* link them to traditions of proletarian literature and to the neglected tradition of Afro-American urban writing as embodied in the work of Wright, Gwendolyn Brooks, and Ann Petry. Zora Neale Hurston, on the other hand, worked for the WPA on the Florida Project. With her anthropological training, she concentrated her literary imagination on evoking a folk past that displaced the context of the rural/urban confrontation in which she wrote. Contemporary critical theory, it seems to me, has likewise produced a discourse that romanticizes the folk roots of Afro-American culture and denies the transformative power of both historical and urban consciousness.

NOTES

1. Charles Davis and Henry Louis Gates, Jr., eds., *The Slave's Narrative* (New York: Oxford University Press, 1985), xiii.

2. Ibid, xxxiii.

3. Pauline Hopkins, *Contending Forces* (Boston: Colored Co-operative Publishing Co., 1900).

4. W. E. B. Du Bois, *The Souls of Black Folk* (Chicago: A. C. McClurg, 1903). This argument could also apply to the early chapters of Du Bois's first novel, *The Quest of the Silver Fleece* (1911; reprint, New York: Arno Press, 1969), and to the figure of Janie's grandmother in Zora Neale Hurston's *Their Eyes Were Watching God* (Philadelphia: J. B. Lippincott, 1937).

5. Houston A. Baker, Jr., *Blues, Ideology, and Afro-American Literature* (Chicago: University of Chicago Press, 1984), 4, 8–9.

6. Hurston, *Their Eyes Were Watching God*, 31–37.

7. Charles H. Nichols, ed., *Arna Bontemps–Langston Hughes Letters, 1925–1967* (New York: Dodd, Mead, 1980), 31, 44, 111, 128; Richard Wright, "Between Laughter and Tears" *New Masses* 25 (October 5, 1937): 22–25. See also Mary Helen Washington, "'I Love the Way Janie Crawford Left Her Husbands': Zora Neale Hurston's Emergent Female Hero," in Washington's *Invented Lives: Narratives of Black Women, 1860–1960* Garden City, N.Y.: Anchor Press, 1987) 237–54.

8. Baker, *Blues, Ideology*, 172–99.

9. Arna Bontemps, *Black Thunder* (1936; reprint, Boston: Beacon Press, 1968); Margaret Walker, *Jubilee* (New York: Bantam, 1966). I make no reference to the following popular novels of slavery: Alex Haley's *Roots*, Frank Yerby's antebellum novels, and the Falconhurst sex and slavery series written by Kyle Onstott, Lance Horner, and Harry Whittington, the best known of which is probably Onstott's *Mandingo*. See Frank Yerby, *The Foxes of Harrow* (New York: Dial Press, 1946), his first and most popular antebellum novel; Alex Haley, *Roots* (Garden City, New York: Doubleday, 1976); Kyle Onstott, *Mandingo* (1957; reprint, Greenwich, Conn.: Fawcett Publications, 1963).

10. Warren I. Susman, *Culture as History* (New York: Pantheon, 1984), 151.

11. My theoretical perspective is influenced by Georg Lukacs, *The Historical Novel* (London: Merlin Press, 1962).

12. Institute for the Black World, "Afterword," in Margaret Walker, *How I Wrote Jubilee* (Chicago: Third World Press, 1977), 29.

13. Ibid.

14. Ibid., 11–12.

15. Richard Harwell, ed., *Margaret Mitchell's Gone with the Wind: Letters, 1936–1949* (New York: Macmillan, 1976), 13.

16. Lukacs, *The Historical Novel*, 84.

17. Susman, *Culture as History*, 106–107.

18. Margaret Mitchell, *Gone with the Wind* (London: Pan Books, 1974), 638–39.

19. For an account of the reactions to McDaniel's performance, see Thomas Cripps, *Slow Fade to Black: The Negro in American Film, 1900–1942* (New York: Oxford University Press, 1977), 359–66.

20. Lukacs, *The Historical Novel*, 77.

21. Ibid., 58.

22. See Hortense J. Spillers, "A Hateful Passion, A Lost Love," *Feminist Studies* 9 (Summer 1983): 293–323. This particular discussion of *Jubilee* is from 298–305.

23. Ibid., 304.

24. See Harriet Jacobs, *Incidents in the Life of a Slave Girl*, ed. Jean Yellin, (Cambridge: Harvard University Press, 1987).

25. See Jerre Mangione, *The Dream and the Deal: The Federal Writer's Project, 1935–1943* (New York: Avon Books, 1972), 124.

26. Walker, *How I Wrote Jubilee*, 27.

27. Ibid., 26.

28. Bontemps, *Black Thunder*.

29. Susman, *Culture as History*, 152.

30. Bontemps, *Black Thunder*, viii, ix, xv.

31. Ibid., x–xi.

32. Ibid., xii.

33. Norman R. Yetman, "Ex-Slave Interviews and the Historiography of Slavery," *American Quarterly* 36 (Summer 1984): 193.

34. Ibid., 195.

35. Bontemps, *Black Thunder*, 148–49.

36. Richard Wright, "A Tale of Folk Courage," *Partisan Review and Anvil* (April 1936): 31.

37. C. L. R. James, *The Black Jacobins: Toussaint L'Ouverture and the San Domingo Revolution* (1938; reprint, London: Allison & Busby, 1980); Herbert Aptheker, *Negro Slave Revolts in the United States, 1526–1860* (New York: International Publishers, 1939). Other revisionist histories published at this time include W. E. B. Du Bois's *Black Reconstruction*, in 1935; Bell Wiley's *Southern Negroes, 1861–1865*, Aptheker's *The Negro in the Civil War*, and Joseph Cephas Carroll's *Slave Insurrections in the United States, 1800–1865*, in 1938; and Harvey Wish's "Slave Disloyalty Under the Confederacy," published in the *Journal of Negro History* in October 1938.

38. James, *The Black Jacobins*, v.

39. Aptheker, *The Negro Slave Revolts*, 3.

40. Ulrich Bonnell Phillips, *Life and Labor in the Old South* (Boston: Little, Brown, 1929).

41. See William Van DeBurg, *Slavery and Race in American Popular Culture* (Madison: University of Wisconsin Press, 1984), 82–85.

42. Ishmael Reed, *Flight to Canada*, (New York: Avon Books, 1976); Sherley Anne Williams, *Dessa Rose* (New York: William Morrow, 1986); David Bradley, *The Chaneysville Incident* (New York: Avon Books, 1981). I would also argue that Toni Morrison's *Beloved* is a remarkable exploration and revisioning of the limits of conventional historical narrative strategies for representing slavery.

43. Bontemps, *Black Thunder*, 9, 224.

44. Ibid., 69.

Deborah E. McDowell

Negotiating between Tenses

WITNESSING SLAVERY AFTER FREEDOM—*DESSA ROSE*

How could she bear witness to what she'd never lived?
—Gayl Jones, *Corregidora*

History is "cannibalistic," and memory becomes the closed arena of
conflict between two contradictory operations: forgetting, an action
directed against the past, and the return of what was forgotten.
—Michael de Certeau, *Heterologies: Discourses on the Other*

Judging from the flood of recent novels about slavery by black
Americans, Ralph Ellison is not amiss in remarking that "the negro
American consciousness is not a product of a will to historical forget-
fulness."[1] The subject of slavery has become a kind of literary "free
for all." And yet, such has not always been the case. The emergence of
what Bernard Bell calls "neoslave narratives"[2] is mainly a post-sixties
phenomenon.[3] Margaret Walker's *Jubilee* (1966) might be chosen arbitrarily as something of a catalyst, for since it was published, novels
about slavery have appeared at an unstoppable rate.[4] Why the compul-
sion to repeat the massive story of slavery in the contemporary Afro-
American novel, especially so long after the empirical event itself? Is
it simply because contemporary writers can "witness" slavery from
the "safe" vantage point of distance? What personal need, what expressive function, does re-presenting slavery in narrative serve the
twentieth-century black American writer? Is the retelling meant to
attempt the impossible: to "get it right," to "set the record straight?"
However one chooses to answer these questions (if one even chooses
to raise them at all), it is certain that these recent fictionalizations of
slavery insert themselves, some by explicit design, into the store of
warring texts, of conflicting interpretations of chattel slavery.[5] Margaret Walker admits that her motivation for writing *Jubilee* was "to set

the record straight where Black people are concerned in terms of the Civil War, of slavery, segregation and Reconstruction."[6]

Like Walker, Sherley Anne Williams suggests that history's lies can be corrected and its omissions, restored. In the "Author's Note" to her novel *Dessa Rose*, Williams admits to "being outraged by a certain, critically acclaimed novel . . . that travestied the as-told-to memoir of slave revolt leader Nat Turner."[7] (Of course, she refers to William Styron's controversial novel *The Confessions of Nat Turner* [1967]).[8] Styron's "meditation on history"[9] is an example of what Williams, in her preface, considers the betrayal of blacks by the written word. Her outrage is understandable considering the repeated scene of blacks' erasure *from* the historical record and their misrepresentation *in* it. But while Williams's "Author's Note" explicitly critiques a novel that allegedly takes history lightly and misrepresents the "known facts" about a black hero—Nat Turner—it licenses itself to do much the same: invent and re-create historical documents. Williams takes two different documented stories—one involving a pregnant black woman who helped to lead a slave revolt in Kentucky, the other concerning a white woman in North Carolina who reportedly gave sanctuary to runaway slaves. Thinking it "sad . . . that these two women never met" in fact, Williams brings them together in fiction. Does Williams's preface reveal a flagrant literary double standard concerning the uses of history in fiction? Does it suggest that it is all right for one writer to take liberties with history and not another? I don't think so.

Dessa Rose stages multiple and often contradictory versions of Dessa's enslavement and subsequent escape, versions that underscore well-rehearsed and commonplace assumptions about the difficulty if not the impossibility of ascertaining the "Truth." And yet the novel resists the pull of the postmodern orthodoxy of undecidability and relativism. In other words, while there might not be one "truth" about Dessa (or about slavery more generally), there are "certainties" that the text stubbornly claims and validates and those it tries to subvert. *Dessa Rose* bears the proud mark of a resolutely propositional and polemical novel, which confronts unabashedly the inescapably ideological contingencies of all discourse, itself included.

Implied in the different versions of Dessa's story are a series of questions connected to the network of sociohistorical realities and power asymmetries that influence the manner and matter of representing slavery. Who has been publically authorized or self-authorized to tell the story? Under what circumstances? What has been acceptably sayable about that story? How have black women been figured in it or figured themselves in it?

It is well known that the majority of published slave narratives were written by black men. According to John Blassingame, black women wrote less than 12 percent of the published slave narratives.[10] From this statistic we can conclude, not surprisingly, that, as autobiography, the slave narratives are primarily expressions of male subjectivity, and, as history, they are narratives of his-story. When black women figure in these male narratives, it is largely as victims of sexual abuse.[11] In this light, it is significant that the majority of contemporary novels about slavery have been written by black women. Moreover, it might be argued that these novels posit a female-gendered subjectivity, more complex in dimension, that dramatizes not what was *done* to slave women, but what they *did* with what was done to them.

Narratives by and about slave women that shift the points of stress from sexual victimization to creative resistance effect an alteration of what can be called a sacred text. Such alterations are common among Afro-American writers in general. William Andrews isolates an example of this pattern in his study of the first century of Afro-American autobiography, or, more popularly, the slave narratives. Andrews is right to read these early narratives as a "a mode of Afro-American scripture" that revised other "culture-defining scriptures," namely, the Bible and the Declaration of Independence.[12] But those black women—both before and after slavery—who have inherited these narratives written predominantly by men have had to revise aspects of this new scripture that, though radical in many ways, has rendered them mere sexual victims.

The concerns that *Dessa Rose* foregrounds—the who, what, when, and how of telling slavery—are richly suggestive and resonate far beyond the imagined scene of that institution which ended in the nineteenth century. This is, to be sure, not a surprising observation considering that what we call the past is merely a function and production of a continuous present and its discourses. We might even argue that it is precisely the "present" and its discourses, in heterogeneous and messy array, that the novel confronts. To choose arbitrarily from its diversely textured field, we can say that the novel engages not only details from inherited texts of slavery but also implicitly questions, comments on, agrees with, and challenges many issues at the forefront of the hydra-headed enterprise (some would say monster) that we loosely term contemporary critical discourse.

It participates aggressively in the critique of the subject and the critique of binary oppositions, both commonly associated with the poststructuralist project. And, with equal vigor, the novel wrestles with questions about the politics and problematics of language and representation. But *Dessa Rose* swerves away from the empty notions of radical indeterminacy that have become the trademark of so much of the discourse at the center of the contemporary critical stage.

It swerves specifically in grounding the oppositions it stages—slavery and freedom, orality and literacy, fact and fiction—in an untidy network of social and material specificities. We might say, finally, that in telling the story of a woman's passage from slavery to freedom, the novel negotiates between past and present to reveal, not surprisingly, that they are not at all discrete. Dessa's is clearly not a progressive evolution from slavery to freedom, for slavery's effects are perdurable even after she has escaped its binding chains. Correspondingly, from the novel I derive my freedom as a reader to negotiate between the "past" and "present" tenses of critical discourse. I want both to "master" the text by telling it and to free it to tell itself, want both to return the text to the world of an assumed reality and to insist that that realm is only a world of words.

I

I know this darky, I tell you; I know her very well.

                                                        —*Dessa Rose*

Just whose "word" can and should be taken in *Dessa Rose* is a question the novel worries in its multiple versions of Dessa's life as a slave. A continuous thread of quotation marks woven throughout the text calls attention to words as words, evoking uncertainty and ambiguity. But then again, this stylization of quotation marks can be said to quarantine misnamings and representations from the implicit textual authority of a counterdiscourse.

The first recorded version of Dessa's story comes from the aptly named Adam (namer) Nehemiah (chronicler) and is littered with words punctuated repetitively with quotation marks. Nehemiah's "authority" as an agent of white male law and rationality is aggressively undermined by the text. His section is a veritable parody of the "as-told-to" device of gathering empirical evidence and documenting events to construct historicist discourse. In his case, Nehemiah is supposedly collecting the facts about Dessa's unrepentant participation in a slave revolt in which many whites were killed. The "facts" that he collects, however, are "some kind of fantastical fiction" (p. 39) recreated in his hand.

The novel compounds the ironies and limitations inherent in Nehemiah's account, which is suspect from the start. It is retrospective, based on discrepant sources, and reconstructed from notes. First, though it purports to be *about* Dessa, a *particular* slave woman, Nehemiah's account actually essentializes Dessa and attempts to fit her into a recognizable proslavery text. His is a representation culled from an inherited store of racist myths about slaves and slavery. "He had been told [slaves] fell asleep much as a cow would in the midst of a satisfying chew," though "he had not observed this himself" (p. 36). And, throughout his chronicle (significantly entitled "Darky," a generic, gender-neutral classification of slaves), Nehemiah admits to being unable to "remember [Dessa's] name" (p. 45). Failing to remember it, he performs a series of substitutions, also lifted from the standard vocabulary of the proslavery text: "darky," "fiend," "devil-woman," "treacherous nigger bitch," "virago," and "she-devil." Although Nehemiah takes notes on the names of slaves that Dessa refers to in her reveries, in his translation they are all reduced to "darky" (p. 39).

Nehemiah's colossal act of serial misnaming mistakes the name for the thing, or, to borrow from Kimberly Benston, it "subsume[s] the complexities of human experience into a tractable sign while manifesting an essential inability to *see* (to grasp, to apprehend) the signified."[13] In telling Dessa's story, Nehemiah creates an abstraction and assigns it a place distant from himself, a distance structured in the novel's use of architectural space(place) and somatophobic imagery. Although Nehemiah conducts his first meeting with Dessa in the root cellar that is her jail, he decides that "being closeted with the darky within the small confines of the cellar was an unsettling experience" (p. 23) and so holds subsequent meetings outside where "he kept a careful distance between them. . . . He would lean forward long enough to wave her to a spot several feet from him, using the vinegar-soaked handkerchief . . . meant to protect him from her scent" (p. 56). These images of smell and verticality (he is *up* in the attic of Hughes's farm house; she is outside it and *down* in the root cellar)[14] signify the physical distance and social inequality between Dessa and Nehemiah that goes far to explain his empowerment but inability to see and to name her.

Hoping to ensure the continued circulation of these performative misnamings and descriptions, Nehemiah is at work on a book on the origins of uprisings among slaves. Commissioned by his publisher Browning Norton, Nehemiah's projected book, *The Roots of Rebellion in the Slave Population and Some Means of Eradicating Them*, exposes his project as a form of slave trading (trading in words) and a tool in the technocratic machinery (he is the son of a mechanic) of social control. But this is no simple story of a black woman's total victimization by that machinery, for Nehemiah proves no match for Dessa.

The narrative symmetrically opposes Nehemiah's public discourse to Dessa's poignant expressions of personal loss and longing. For every question he wants answered with facts about the uprising— "Where were the renegades going?" "Who were the darkies that got away?" (p. 36)—Dessa answers with some memory of Kaine's confrontation with the slave system or by singing a song. Throughout their sessions, she cleverly misleads him and mocks what he represents. And in the studied circularity of her telling (leading Nehemiah back to the same point of previous sessions) and her skill at "turn[ing] his . . . questions back upon themselves," Dessa sabotages his enterprise. Her confessed enjoyment of "play[ing] on his words" sends him scrambling to write "quickly, abbreviating with a reckless abandon, scribbling almost as he sought to keep up with the flow of her words" (p. 60). Her refusal to "confess" anything to Nehemiah that would facilitate yet another misrepresentation is an act of resistance against the adverse power of literacy and codification. At novel's end Nehemiah's "book" is incomplete; it has literally fallen apart and is nothing more than loose pages "scatter[ed] about the floor," unreadable scribbling that even the sheriff (another agent of the father's law) cannot read. Further, Nehemiah's own name has been abbreviated; he is "Nemi" and has *become* the reduction he would create.

II

The evidence of things not seen.

—Heb. 11:1

Can we identify a work of art . . . if it does not bear the mark of a genre?

—Derrida, "The Law of Genre"

That misnaming is generative is a point graphically illustrated in section two of *Dessa Rose*. In escaping from Nehemiah, Dessa seizes physical freedom, but she does not escape the text of slavery. She continues to be misnamed and performs her own misnaming. We might say that sections 1 and 2 juxtapose two consubstantial systems of representation—one is verbal; the other, visual. Told largely from the point of view of Rufel, a white woman, this second section is structured on the language of the visual that she employs while remembering her own past and her own complicity in and victimization by the institution of slavery.

Whereas the first section is based on a series of opposition—of orality and literacy, of public and private discourse, of a free white male and an enslaved black woman—the second problematizes "the whole business of choosing sides" (p. 78) and moves toward an ethic and an energy of cooperation. That ethic is most readily apparent in the links established between Dessa and Rufel, an escaped slave and a one-time slave mistress. Both are separated from their families; both are mourning personal losses; both are raising children; both live under a system that denies either full control over her body. But these commonalities are produced by radically different material circumstances and thus engender radically different effects.

While Rufel's section uses the problem of naming and representation to attempt to bridge the "schism in the sisterhood"[15] between black and white women, it neither simplifies that process nor attempts to merge their differences and make them the same. It makes a difference that one woman is white and the other is black. The process of transgressing their oppositions and antagonisms and the impregnable social boundaries that separate them begins with efforts to get out of the text of slavery that both misname and mis-see.

As slave mistress in action, if not in fact, Rufel replicates and extends Nehemiah's practice of essentializing slaves and consigning them to places. Whereas his section is entitled "Darky"—a gender-neutral nomination— Rufel's is titled "Wench," a female-specific nomination, but one no closer to naming Dessa Rose. True to her trade as a caricaturist, Rufel has an exaggerated and distorted image of Dessa and the other escaped slaves harbored on her rundown plantation, forcing them to fit a different sacred text: the visual image of slaves produced and reproduced in nineteenth century popular culture. Rufel

associates Ada with "the stock cuts used to illustrate newspaper adver-
tisements of slave sales and runaways: pants rolled up to the knees,
bareheaded, a bundle attached to a stick slung over one shoulder, the
round white eyes in the inky face" (p. 140). Coming close upon Nathan at the shoreline, "she turned to the darky aghast. . . . Never had
she seen such blackness. She . . . expect[ed] to see the bulbous lips and
bulging eyes of a burnt-cork minstrel" but saw instead "a pair of rather
shadowy eyes and strongly defined features that were— handsome" (p.
125). Finally, as she remembers her faithful servant, Mammy, whose
death she mourns, Rufel performs another familiar substitution, visu-
alizing Mammy's "cream-colored bandanna," the traditional sign of
the slave woman's servitude. She corrects that memory by recalling
that "the silky-looking cloth on the darky's head bore little resemblance to the gaudy-colored swatch most darkies tied about their
heads. This was a scarf, knotted in a rosette behind one ear" (p. 123).
These passages suggest that, while Rufel seems able to adjust her
vision of these slaves, she cannot right their names, not even
"Mammy," the name of the slave woman she professes to love.

Significantly, it is over Rufel's misnaming Mammy that she and
Dessa have their first major confrontation, and their mutual misnam-
ing is a source of continual difficulty and mistrust between the two
women. As Rufel fits Mammy into her largely idealized memories of
her life as a Southern belle in Charleston, Dessa bursts out,
"'Mammy' ain't nobody name, not they real one" (p. 119). Dessa forces
Rufel to see that if she didn't know Mammy's name, she didn't know
Mammy. Even the most basic details about Mammy are unknown to
Rufel, who is left to wonder in hindsight: "Had Mammy minded
when the family no longer called her name? . . . How old *had*
Mammy been? . . . Had she any children?" (p. 129)

Though the confrontation between Rufel and Dessa over
"Mammy" is painful to them both, it puts each in touch with the buried aspects of her past and initiates the process of intimacy and trust.
That process is figured in the poetics of space and architecture. Whereas Nehemiah's section employs images of vertical space to underscore
the *distance* between him and Dessa, Rufel's uses images of horizontal

space to figure the possibility of *closeness* between the two women.

Rufel's Sutton's Glen is a down-at-the-heels plantation. Its "BIG HOUSE" consists of two large rooms and a lean-to kitchen. Significantly, it has no second floor. The slave "Quarters" consist of "one room with a dirt floor" (p. 165) with a side for women and one for men (p. 116). This spatial configuration is used to abrogate the hierarchies of place, the divisions in the social order that place Rufel on top and Dessa below. Brought to Sutton's Glen, weak and delirious from childbirth, Dessa is taken to Rufel's bedroom and placed in her bed. While the bed (implying no necessary eroticization), becomes the symbolic site of mediation between these two women, working to mitigate their mutual suspicion and distrust, only mutual acts of imagination and self-projection can strengthen the bridge.

The burden of initiation falls largely on Rufel, who maintains a place of privilege and power despite her own victimization by the slave system. For example, according to the laws and customs governing southern race relations, Rufel's *word* is equivalent to truth. As Ada says, "White woman ain't got no excuse to be trifling when all it take is they word" (p. 176), a point made clearly evident when Dessa is temporarily recaptured. It is Rufel's word, as a Southern Lady, even in the form of a disguise, that helps to free Dessa for the last time, underscoring Rufel's power over Dessa's life, her body, her story.

While Rufel can shelter Dessa, she cannot believe that Dessa has been physically abused. Consistent with her attachment to the visual as well as her need for entertainment, Rufel wants to *hear* Dessa's story and *see* the visual "evidence," but Dessa, also suspicious, refuses to comply. The narrative that Rufel hears of Dessa's abuse is mediated, coming secondhand from Nathan. Rufel disbelieves the story, because she sees no scars on Dessa's back. When Nathan explains that they are on her hips and thighs, Rufel asks: "How do you know?" Clearly, Rufel needs "to see them scars before she would buy the story" (p. 189). "How else was she to know the truth of what they said?" For Rufel "seeing is believing"; to see is to know, a point raising questions about the recent feminist discourse that associates "looking," or the "gaze," with the masculine, dissociating it from the particularity of race and social location. Rufel's eye objectifies and stabilizes the slaves at Sutton's Glen, a practice linked to her *racial* privilege.[16] References to slaves averting their gazes and lowering their lashes in her presence figure throughout Rufel's narrative (pp. 134, 139, 143).

In order for any distance to be bridged between Rufel and Dessa, then, Rufel must suspend the notion that only visual, empirical evidence can verify the truth of Dessa's abuse. She must rely on her imagination, instead, the act not of objectifying but of identifying with, or getting into, another's place. As she listens to Nathan recount Dessa's story, Rufel "could almost feel the fire that must have lived in the wench's thighs," the "branding iron searing tender flesh" (p. 138). She expresses disgust at "that vicious trader," "to violate a body so" (p. 135). She asks sympathetically, "How did they bare such pain?" (p. 138), but, importantly, she uses "bare" (again suggesting the visual) not "bear."

Significantly, Rufel hears this story not from Dessa herself, but from Nathan. Dessa has avoided this public exposure as fiercely as she has hidden her bodily scars. To expose them is to expose the horrors of victimization, to participate symbolically in a slave auction—to be publically exhibited, displayed. Further, this "history writ about her privates" (p. 21) is a script written in the slave master's hand and bound up in his enslaving psychosexual myths and fantasies. Here, Dessa's body is *her* text and, owning it, she holds the rights to it. For Dessa, concealing the story from Rufel is just that—a radical act of ownership over her own body/text in a system that successfully stripped slaves' control over this, their most intimate property. Because Dessa perceives Rufel's physical relationship with Nathan as theft of a possession,[17] it is no wonder that she wants to own her story. Additionally, to publicize this "history writ about her privates" is synonymous with baring a past too painful to bear.

III

The future was a matter of keeping the past at bay.
                                        —Toni Morrison, *Beloved*

Dessa's refusal to confess the intimate details of her life to either Nehemiah or Rufel is both an act of resistance (she is the repository of her own story) and a means of containing her pain by forgetting the past. Her refusal to "confess" to Nehemiah and Rufel is understandable, but Dessa is no more able to speak about her past in the atmosphere of trust and caring that obtains among the escaped slaves at Rufel's Glen. "Even when the others spoke around the campfire, during the days of their freedom, about their trials under slavery, Dessa was silent. . . . That part of the past lay sealed in the scars between her thighs" (pp. 59–60). But, like so many Afro-American novels, *Dessa Rose* links getting "beyond" slavery to remembering it, paradoxically burying it and bearing it, a process exemplified in the naming of Dessa's baby. Consistent with her desire to bury the past, Dessa rejects Nathan's suggestion to name the baby after Kaine, his father. "The baby's daddy, like that part of her life, was dead; she would not rake it up each time she called her son's name." And so she wants to name the baby for the men who rescued her from Nehemiah. Rufel (again, possessed of the power to "name") strikes a compromise by suggesting a name that incorporates both tenses: "Desmond Kaine"–"Des" for Odessa, "mond" to represent the men . . . who were responsible for his free birth" (p. 148), and "Kaine" to represent the past.

The child is the evidence that forgetting the past cannot be willed so easily. "Even buried under the years of silence [she] could not forget," but she chooses to undergo the process of remembering in the presence of other slaves. When she does begin to tell her story in her own voice, in the final section of the novel, she tells it first and mainly to an audience of black women—a dominant pattern in Afro-American women's fiction—which points to the delicate relationship between teller and listener, writer and audience, in the establishment of textual authority.

Although Dessa slowly develops trust for Rufel, it is and can only be a partial trust: "I'd catch myself about to tell . . . some little thing, like I would Carrie or Martha. . . . She did ask about that coffle and scaping out that celler. I told her some things, how they chained us, the way the peoples sang in the morning at the farm. But I wouldn't talk about Kaine, about the loss of my peoples. . . . So we didn't talk too much that was personal" (p. 216). It should be noted, here, that Dessa does not share confidences with Rufel, only details of a collective, historical record, details in the public domain, if you will.

This is the difficult and precarious balance that contemporary novels about slavery must strike—that between the public record and private memory, between what Bakhtin calls "authoritative discourse" ("privileged language that . . . permits no play with its framing context [Sacred Writ, for example]") and "internally-persuasive discourse . . . which is more akin to retelling a text in one's own words."[18] Bakhtin's distinction coordinates roughly with the polarity between Nehemiah's discourse and Dessa's. The novel plots the progressive movements away from Nehemiah's *written* "authoritative discourse" within which Dessa is framed (with all of the multiple valences of that term), and the emergence of Dessa's own story, *spoken* without Nehemiah's mediation in her own words, and with her own inflections. To borrow from William Andrews, Dessa tells a "free story."[19]

Let me rush to insert here that I do not mean to suggest (nor, I believe, does the novel) that because Dessa must *speak* her text rather than *write* it, it is therefore ipso facto "freer" and without mediation or that she is necessarily always self-present and thus has a higher claim to truth. Dessa's story is mediated, largely by the operations of memory, but the suggestion is that, by virtue of her social and material circumstances, her version of her story must be seen as more reliable than Nehemiah's could ever be. Moreover, in Dessa's section, the initial sharply drawn distinction between orality and literacy is complicated by its recontextualization. Removed from the site of enslavement and oppression, the notion of "writing" is expanded and linked to speech.[20] That complication is structured in Dessa's acquisition and use of the language of literacy, apparent in her repeated use of writing metaphors. Thinking back on her life with Kaine, Dessa expresses gladness that Kaine "wasn't Master, wasn't boss," adding that "these wasn't peoples *in my book*" (p. 184; my emphasis). Similarly, when she comes upon Nathan and Rufel making love, she fixes on the stark contrast between his blackness and the surrounding whiteness—"white sheets, white pillows, white bosom." "He wasn't nothing but a *mark* on them." From there, she generalizes about black-white relations: "That's what we was in white folk eyes, nothing but marks to be used, wiped out" (p. 171). Though illiterate, Dessa understands the functional quality of language. She notices that, in organizing the flimflam scheme, Harker, also illiterate, "made up some marks that wasn't writing but he used it like that" (p. 195). Finally free to wander about town during one of the stops on the flimflam trail, Dessa indulges her fascination with the printer's shop: "I couldn't see that printing machine often enough to suit me" (p. 215), she says. And in a final gesture that valuates the written word, Dessa wants her story recorded (p. 236), but, importantly, she invests herself with the power and authority to validate it, for she has her son "say it back" (p. 236) after he has written it.

IV

Blow up the law, break up the "truth" with laughter.
—Helene Cixous, "The Laugh of the Medusa"

In the text that Dessa authorizes her son to tell, she particularizes her experiences within more familiar generic conventions of slavery. "I was spared much that others suffered" (p. 176), she says (specifically, sexual abuse and sales on the auction block). More, unlike the familiar story of slavery, especially that told in antebellum slave narratives, the inflection of laughter dominates Dessa's text, and, I must add, it is not the laughter fabricated in plantation myths of the happy darky strumming on the old banjo. It is, rather, the laughter implied in Cixous's "The Laugh of the Medusa"—"law-breaking" laughter, "truth-breaking laughter," or as Henri Bergson describes, "everything that comes under the heading of 'topsyturvydom.'" According to Bergson, comedy frequently sets before us a character ensnared in his own trap— "the villain who is the victim of his own villainy, or the cheat cheated." In every case, he concludes, "the root idea involves an inversion of the roles, and a situation which recoils on the head of its author."[21]

In Dessa's story, which is largely the account of a well-oiled scam, she and her comrades turn the "authoritative" texts of slavery back on themselves. They use all the recognizable signs of those texts but strip them of their meaning and power. These escaped slaves contrive to repeatedly sell themselves back into slavery only to escape again. They exploit Southern law and custom and faithfully enact the narrow roles it assigns slaves and women. Dessa plays the "Mammy"; Rufel, the "Mistress"; and Nathan, her "Nigger driver." Allowing for the ever-present threat of discovery, they plan, if captured, for Dessa and the other slaves to "act dumb and scared," while Rufel is "to act high-handed and helpless" (p. 194). In other words, they re-enter a familiar script and enact the roles it assigns, roles misread and misrecognized, as is classically demonstrated when Dessa is indeed recaptured by Nehemiah. He drags her to the jail and alleges that she is an escaped slave matching the description on a reward poster: "Dark complexed. Spare built. Shows the whites of her eyes—" (p. 222). When the sheriff responds that the description "sound like about twenty negroes [he] knows personally" (p. 222), Nehemiah orders Dessa to show her scars. From here Dessa has Southern gentility and patriarchy on her side. Both Nehemiah and the sheriff stand up when Rufel enters the room and inveighs against scandalous people who "prey on defenseless womens" (p. 226). Batting her eyes, she suggests that Nehemiah has simply mistaken Dessa for someone else. This gives Dessa confidence that the sheriff "couldn't take [Nehemiah's] word against the word of a respectable white lady" (p. 225), especially not in a dispute over something *down there*. "Cept for them scars, it was the word of a crazy white man against a respectable white lady" (p. 226). In this system, Nehemiah's recourse is to *ask* Rufel if she would lie for Dessa. He cannot *accuse* her of lying, because a "white man ain't posed to call no white lady a lie" (p. 227). The slave woman summoned to check Dessa's scars likewise denies that she has any. Ironically, then, the "evidence" the law uses to support its judgment to free Dessa comes not from Nehemiah, but from two women. More important, Dessa, who learned early on that "a nigger can't talk before the laws, not against no white man" (p. 49) and who admitted at one time that she had "no idea what a 'court' was (p. 55), stands before the sheriff, the servant of the law, and Nehemiah, one of its arch-defenders, and pleads her case. These women, all three victimized by Southern patriarchy and its racial and sexual politics, find a power within that system by turning it back on itself, by turning its assumptions about blacks and women topsy-turvy.

And, except for that narrow escape, they have fun in the process, calling up "the comical things happened on the [flimflam] trail" (p. 216). As Dessa says, "We laughed so we wouldn't cry; we was seeing ourselfs as we had been and seeing the thing that had made us. Only way we could defend ourselves was by making it into some hair-raising story or a joke" (p. 208). She continues, "I told myself this was good, that it showed slavery didn't have no hold on us no more" (p. 213).

V

Am I suggesting something as outlandish (to say nothing of morally repugnant) as that Dessa's story would have us see that slavery was an institution to be laughed at, laughed about, laughed over? Clearly not. This is no book of "laughter and forgetting," to pinch from Milan Kundera, no dramatization of the thesis that slavery was not really "so bad" after all. It clearly was, and the historical record on that score is well known. For nearly four centuries, millions of human beings were kidnapped, some willingly sold into bondage by their own kin, and transported across the ocean to provide the labor power that made the misnamed "Peculiar Institution." But these all-too-well-known horrific details were not the whole story, as such historians as John Blassingame, Eugene Genovese, Herbert Gutman, and Deborah Gray White have done well to establish.

Contemporary Afro-American writers who tell a story of slavery are increasingly aiming for the same thing: to reposition the stress points of that story with a heavy accent on particular acts of agency within an oppressive and degrading system. In a recent interview that followed the publication of *Beloved*, Toni Morrison explains that slavery was "so intricate, so immense and so long, and so unprecedented," that it can take the writer over. She adds, "we know what that story is. And it is predictable." The writer must, then, focus not on the institution but on the people, which puts the "authority back into the hands of the slave."[22]

To repeat, Dessa Rose is the final authority on her story, controlling her own text. But controlling a text of slavery, or any other text for that matter, especially a written one, is no guarantee of freedom. Triumph over language does not translate directly into triumph over social and material circumstances. The novel establishes this point most clearly after Dessa has escaped Nehemiah for the final time. Dessa and Rufel walk about the town of Arcopolis (an anagram of Acropolis?), with all the associations of logocentrism and law (polis), and yet what has developed between these two women is a threat to both the word and the law. They have threatened this system by challenging if not escaping from its terms. They free themselves from the mutual antagonism and distrust, the name-calling that assigns each a confining place and role. As they walk along, Dessa, now accustomed to calling Rufel "Mis'ess," addresses her as such. Rufel answers, "I ain't your mistress. My name is Ruth." In a reciprocal gesture that reclaims her own "proper name," Dessa answers, "My name Dessa, Dessa Rose. Ain't no O to it" (p. 232).

Dessa wants to hug Ruth at this point but hugs Rufel's daughter instead. Throughout the novel their children have functioned both to mediate and mollify the differences between them and to symbolize the possibilities of a new order.[23] We can say that *Dessa Rose*, and other contemporary novels of slavery, witnesses slavery after freedom in order to engrave that past on the memory of the present but, more importantly, on future generations that might otherwise succumb to the cultural amnesia that has begun to re-enslave us all in social and literary texts that impoverish our imaginations.

NOTES

1. Ralph Ellison, William Styron, Robert Penn Warren, and C. Vann Woodward, "The Uses of History in Fiction," *Southern Literary Journal* 1 (Spring 1969): 60.

2. Bernard W. Bell, *The Afro-American Novel and Its Tradition* (Amherst: University of Massachusetts Press, 1987), 289. Henry Louis Gates terms the form the "slave narrative novel." See "The Language of Slavery," his introduction to *The Slave's Narrative*, ed. Charles Davis and Henry L. Gates, Jr. (New York: Oxford University Press, 1985).

3. Of course, there were novels of slavery published before the 1960s, but, in terms of sheer numbers, it is a subject engaged by far more authors of this century. Nineteenth-century novels of slavery include the major antebellum novels—William Wells Brown's *Clotel; or the President's Daughter: A Narrative of Slave Life in the United States* (1853); Martin Delaney's *Blake; or the Huts of America* (1859) and Harriet E. Wilson's *Our Nig* (1859); James Howard's *Bond and Free* (1866); and, though not focused exclusively on slavery, Frances E. W. Harper's *Iola Leroy* (1892). Twentieth-century examples include Arna Bontemp's historical romances, *Black Thunder* (1936) and *Drums at Dusk* (1939). See Hazel Carby's essay "Ideologies of Black Folk: The Historical Novel of Slavery" in this volume for a discussion of what she describes as a paradox. She argues that, though it is "central to the Afro-American literary imagination . . . as a mode of production and as a particular social order, slavery is rarely the focus of the imaginative physical and geographical terrain of Afro-American novels."

4. Recent novels about slavery include Ernest Gaines's *The Autobiography of Miss Jane Pittman* (1971), Ishmael Reed's *Flight to Canada* (1976), Barbara Chase-Riboud's *Sally Hemings* (1979), Octavia Butler's *Kindred* (1979), Charles Johnson's *The Oxherding Tale* (1982), Sherley Anne Williams's *Dessa Rose* (1984), and Toni Morrison's *Beloved* (1987). Even those recent novels by black

Americans which do not focus exclusively on slavery or use it as a significant point of departure, stage characters' necessary confrontation with some story about slavery. Examples include Avey in Paul Marshall's *Praisesong for the Widow* (1983) and Ursa in Gayl Jones's *Corregidora* (1975).

5. For a general survey of the history of these warring interpretations see William L. Van Deburg, *Slavery and Race in American Popular Culture* (Madison: University of Wisconsin Press, 1984).

6. See Charles Rowell, "Poetry, History, and Humanism: Interview with Margaret Walker," *Black World*, December 1975, #10.

7. Sherley Anne Williams, "Author's Note" to *Dessa Rose* (New York: William Morrow, 1986), 5. All further references to the novel are to the first edition and given in parentheses in the text and notes.

8. The controversy surrounding Styron's novel was widespread among black writers and intellectuals, most of whom maintained that Styron's imagined Nat Turner bore little resemblance to the actual historical figure. See *William Styron's Nat Turner: Ten Black Writers Respond*, ed. John Henrik Clarke (Boston: Beacon Press, 1968). And for a critique of Styron's critics see Seymour L. Gross and Eileen Bender, "History, Politics, and Literature: The Myth of Nat Turner," *American Quarterly* 23 (October 1971): 487–518.

9. A version of the first section of *Dessa Rose* entitled "Meditations on History," no doubt an act of signifying on Styron's description of his novel, appeared in *Midnight Birds: Stories of Contemporary Black Women Writers* (New York: Anchor/Doubleday, 1980), 200–248.

10. See "Using the Testimony of Ex-Slaves: Approaches and Problems" in *The Slave's Narrative*, ed. Charles Davis and Henry L. Gates, Jr. (New York: Oxford, 1985),83.

11. Frances Foster notes that in the published slave narratives that black women contributed to the genre, their sexual abuse is noticeably deemphasized. She observes that they "never present rape or seduction as the most profound aspect of their existence" ("'In Respect to Females . . .': Differences in the Portrayals of Women by Male and Female Narrators," *Black American Literature Forum*, 15 [Summer 1981]: 67).

12. William L. Andrews, *To Tell a Free Story: The First Century of Afro-American Autobiography, 1760–1865* (Urbana: University of Illinois Press, 1986), 14.

13. "'I yam, what I am': The Topos of Un(naming) in Afro-American Literature," in *Black Literature and Literary Theory*, ed. Henry Louis Gates, Jr. (New York: Methuen, 1984), 157.

14. Williams also uses architectural space/place to ironize and mock Nehemiah's assumed superiority, for his "Big House" is Hughes's rundown farmhouse in which he has an "'attic half' that was little better than a loft" (p. 26), a far cry from the "Great Houses" of cavalier Virginia that had once opened their doors to him.

15. I borrow this phrase from Margaret A. Simons, "Racism and Feminism: A Schism in the Sisterhood," *Feminist Studies* 5 (Summer 1979): 384–401.

16. For a discussion of the feminist interrogation and critique of gender-linked vision see Craig Owens, "The Discourse of Others: Feminists and Post-modernism," in *The Anti-Aesthetic: Essays on Post-Modern Culture*, ed. Hal Foster (Port Townsend, Wash.: Bay Press, 1983), 57–77, esp. 70–77.

17. Dessa describes to Harker, "White folks had taken everything in the world from me except my baby and my life and they had tried to take them. And to see him, who had helped to save me, had friended with me . . . laying up, wallowing in what had hurt me so—I didn't feel that nothing I could say would tell him what that pain was like" (p. 173).

18. M. M. Bakhtin, *The Dialogic Imagination*, ed. Michael Holquist (Austin: University of Texas Press, 1981), 424.

19. See Andrews, *To Tell a Free Story.*

20. In an important and influential essay, "The Blues Roots of Contemporary Afro-American Poetry," Williams states that "the beginning of a new tradition" of Afro-American literature is "built on a synthesis of black oral traditions and Western literate forms" (*Massachusetts Review*, 17 [Autumn 1977]: 554).

21. Henri Bergson, *Comedy* (New York: Doubleday, 1956), 121–22.

22. Toni Morrison, interview by Charlayne Hunter-Gault, "MacNeil/Lehrer Report," September 29, 1987.

23. Some would say that the "new order" *Dessa Rose* imagines is utopian and idealized. For example, in a recent review of Gloria Naylor's novel *Mama Day*, David Nicholson criticizes *Dessa Rose* for "retreating into an imaginary past" (see "Gloria Naylor's Island of Magic and Romance," *Washington Post Book World*, February 28, 1988).

Library of Congress Cataloging-in-Publication Data

Slavery and the literary imagination.

   (Selected papers from the English Institute, 1987;
new ser., no. 13)
   Bibliography: p.
   1. American literature—19th century—History
and criticism.   2. Slavery and slaves in literature.
3. Afro-Americans in literature.   4. American
literature—20th century—History and criticism.
5. American literature—20th century—History and
criticism.   I. McDowell, Deborah E., 1951– .
II. Rampersad, Arnold.   III. Series: Selected papers
from the English Institute; new ser., no. 13.
PS217.S55S55 1989   810′.9′3520625   88-45405
ISBN 0-8018-3756-1 (alk. paper)
ISBN 0-8018-3948-3 (pbk.)